C.I.I.S
March 1998

For Lawrence,

A Western Approac

Reincarnation and Karma

who knows about
such things!
Warmly,
Robert McD.

Vista Series

Volume 2

A Western Approach to Reincarnation and Karma

Selected Lectures and Writings by Rudolf Steiner

Edited and Introduced by

René Querido

Anthroposophic Press

Published by Anthroposophic Press
RR 4 Box 94 A1, Hudson, NY 12534

The lectures in this book are translated b y Catherine E. Creeger from the Collected Work of Rudolf Steiner, published by Rudolf Steiner Verlag, Dornach, Switzerland, as follows: 1. from vol. 120, *Die Offenbarungen des Karma*, Lecture 5, "Natürliche und zufällige Erkkrankungen in Beziehung zu Karma"; 2. from vol. 120, Lecture 7, "Elementarereignisse, Vulkanausbrüche, Erdbeben, Epidemien in Beziehung zu Karma"; 3. from vol. 120, Lecture 9, "Tod und Gebeurt im Verhältnis zu Karma; 4. from vol. 135, *Wiederverkörperung und Karma*, Lecture 4; 5. from vol. 135, Lecture 5; 6. from vol. 125, *Wege und Ziele des geistigen Menschen,* Lecture 11; 7. from vol. 235, *Esoterische Betrachtungen karmischer Zusammenhänge (Erster Band)*, Lecture 4; 8. from vol. 9, *Theosophie, Einführung in übersinnliche Welterkenntnis und Menschenbestimmung*, Chapter 2.

LIBRARY OF CONGRESS CATALOGING-IN-PUBLICATION DATA

Steiner, Rudolf, 1861–1925.
[Lectures. English. Selections]
A Western approach to reincarnation and karma : lectures / by Rudolf Steiner ; introduction by René Querido.
p. cm. — (Vista series)
Includes bibliographical references (p. 139) and index.
ISBN 0-88010-399-X (paper)
1. Anthroposophy. 2. Reincarnation. 3. Karma. 4. Christianity and reincarnation. I. Querido, René M., 1926– . II. Title. III. Series.
BP596.R44S74213 1996
299'935—dc20 95-43107
CIP

10 9 8 7 6 5 4 3 2 1

Printed in the United States of America

Contents

The Vista Series

FOREWORD BY ROBERT MCDERMOTT

A full century after he introduced his methods for the attainment of spiritual knowledge and for cultural renewal, Rudolf Steiner's anthroposophy offers spiritual practices and esoteric insights relevant for the most vexing problems facing humanity at this time. The many thousands who are attempting to implement his spiritual-scientific method often express surprise and frustration that his influence has not been more widely felt in academic, scientific, and artistic circles. Part of the reason for this neglect is surely that Steiner offers neither simple answers nor a simple method. He repeatedly cautioned his followers and readers not to accept his research as answers, but rather to conduct their own spiritual-scientific research and, in the process, to check and advance his esoteric indications.

Another reason for the neglect of Steiner's research is simply that his insights are scattered throughout three hundred volumes. It would take a lifetime of reading to know where to find many or most of Steiner's ideas on any one theme, and a lifetime of careful sorting to know why Steiner shifted his observations from one set of lectures to another. Because he was developing neither a system of categories nor an encyclopedia of answers, but rather an experimental approach to the inner realities of the material and spiritual worlds, he repeatedly returned to complex themes in order to explore them from diverse angles and in diverse contexts.

The "Vista Series" attempts to make more available to the general reader Steiner's spiritual-scientific methodology and its results concerning major themes in the arts, sciences, social sciences, and education. Each volume will include selections from Steiner's writings and lectures accompanied by extensive introductory material by an editor who combines an expertise in the theme of the book and a thorough familiarity with the full range of Steiner's published works. These volumes are intended for a general reader interested in a spiritual-scientific approach to such topics as nature, visual arts, education, philosophy, higher beings, such as Krishna and Buddha, evolution of consciousness, social and economic life, and gender. The ideal approach to these volumes, and to Steiner's spiritual teaching generally, is to be open yet discerning, spiritual and esoteric yet truly empirical.

With one exception, all of the problems that Rudolf Steiner attempted to solve, and all of the spiritual-esoteric questions that he researched, he undertook in response to requests from colleagues facing real challenges in their lived situations. The one exception, the one work that Steiner took upon himself on his own initiative, is the subject of this volume, the double concept of karma and reincarnation. Steiner considered it to be an essential part of his own karma to enable the West, particularly the Christian West, to accept and work with a modern Western version of karma and reincarnation. Throughout these pages—and many hundreds of pages not included in this volume—Steiner recommends that modern Western individuals should strive spiritually to penetrate the mysterious dynamics of karma and rebirth in a way that affirms individual freedom and fosters cultural renewal.

• • •

These volumes have been generously supported by a grant from Laurance S. Rockefeller, a philanthropist intensely conscious of the mysteries and diverse meanings of his own biography and the biographies of the many new or spiritually-experimental paradigm thinkers whose work he has assisted through his commitment to a deeper and more integrated understanding of body, mind, and spirit.

ROBERT McDERMOTT
Series Editor

Introduction

BY RENÉ QUERIDO

1.
Our Present Dilemma

Conflict in the Modern Soul

Ideas of reincarnation and karma have been more widespread in the Western world than one might at first imagine. They have risen to popularity, especially during the last thirty years, due in large measure to New Age impulses that value alternative views, and embrace concepts and practices of various Eastern religions, among others. Most philosophies and religions in the West strongly oppose the idea of karma and rebirth; the ingrained materialism of our society denies spiritual values altogether, including ideas of re-embodiment. Moreover, fundamentalist Christian groups reject the notion of reincarnation, mainly on the grounds that it is not mentioned in the Bible. Some people are vaguely familiar with reincarnation and karma in a general way, but do not understand how re-embodiment works or what karma means.

Rudolf Steiner (1861–1925), philosopher, seer, educator, artist for about twenty-one years at the beginning of the century, presented remarkable teachings about reincarnation and karma. What he said enables any person on a path to the spirit to understand reincarnation and karma through thinking, to sense their reality in feeling, and to apply this knowledge in everyday life in a practical way. How this is so will be elaborated in this introduction, and the extracts chosen from Steiner's vast work will bear testimony to it.

Fundamental Soul Questions

Sooner or later a human being who awakens to the outer world and to a consciousness of the inner self will encounter the following major life questions:

> *Who am I?*—the question of identity.
> *What is the significance of my relationship to other human beings, whether relatives, loved ones, friends, or co-workers?*—the question of destiny.
> *Does life on Earth have any purpose? Do I have a task in life?*—the question of meaning.

Today, as traditions, conventions, and values increasingly break down, the alienated human being senses these questions in an existential way, a way both poignant and painful. We are not merely entertaining philosophical ideas, but matters of life and death for the soul.

Of course, there are ways of escaping this starkness: alcohol, drugs, and self-indulgences of all kinds can for a time obscure these crucial questions of the soul. Others may find comfort in old forms and rituals, even if performed with a clear understanding of their true meaning. Such involvements might appease the heart and lull the soul into drowsiness, but the underlying abyss remains and one is never entirely unaware of it. Various forms of inner and outer anxiety are often what eventually prompt the soul to embark on a quest to resolve the apparent inexplicability of life on Earth.

Identity and Destiny

The question of identity arises in many ways. A nine-year-old child (or even younger) may awaken one day and suddenly realize the *I*, the self, unique and different from every other human being, including family. This can be a shattering experience, because it marks the beginning of a chasm between self and world, and is felt very strongly with the onset of puberty, possibly resulting in the soul feeling alienated: "I am different"— "I am not understood"— "I do not feel at home in this world, and yet people tell me that I belong here."[1] These discoveries can easily turn a young person into a loner, brooding deeply on his or her own true nature; or lead to a longing for escape, to mix aimlessly with others in endless distraction in order to forget the pain of becoming an individual in the world.

Yet, this transition can also be the beginning of an intensive quest in which, little by little, the soul realizes: Although I am the result of procreation, and the forces of heredity have formed my physical body, I am a unique individual. The realization that there is more to life than a biological past can further awaken the awareness of a distinction between *personality* and *individuality*. My personality — from the Latin word *persona*, which means "mask" — is the product of my heredity and environment. One might say that it represents the everyday self. Yet, I am also the result of a spiritual past, a unique individuality that appears veiled and dormant when compared to its full potential.

So, one might come to the thought of two selves: one that is unique and eternal—a better self—and another transient self, fettered to and conditioned by the realities of birth and death. The experience of this dichotomy can produce a dramatic tension in a modern soul in quest of its own reality. We might experience the thought expressed by Wordsworth in his "Imitations of Immortality," where he speaks of the life of the soul before entering into physical existence:

> Our birth is but a sleep and a forgetting;
> The soul that rises with us, our life's star,
> Hath had elsewhere its setting,
> And cometh from afar.

---

1. See, for example, Rudolf Steiner, *The Child's Changing Consciousness As the Basis of Pedagogical Practice*, Anthroposophic Press, Hudson, NY, 1996.

We find that modern science, as well as some Christian denominations, arrive at very different answers to this fundamental question about each human being. Modern biological sciences attempt to explain the nature of the human being in a purely materialistic way, that our life on Earth is the result of biological processes of procreation, and that complexities related to our genes make us what we are—creatures of flesh and blood, produced by heredity, and evolved from a previous animal condition.

Do these explanations satisfy the innermost core of our being, and help us to deal with our deepest anxieties? These important questions are all too often shoved aside with the question: Can you prove it scientifically?

A number of religions are built on the conviction that God created us at conception, out of nothing, and pre-existence is not even a consideration. Even the religious proposition that life continues in another form after death usually lacks clarity and fails to offer much solace, nor does it usually make much difference in the way daily life is lived and experienced.

For many contemporary men and women, even those who long for something more, the landscape of the inner soul life is much like a desert. Friedrich Nietzsche was perhaps the first to use the phrase, "God is dead." It is certainly strange and distressing that some Protestant theologians took up Nietzsche's phrase with conviction. Whether we struggle with nihilism or not, as modern souls we can understand the words of the theologian Paul Tillich: "The anxiety of emptiness and meaninglessness is dominant. We are under the threat of spiritual non-being."

Clearly this question concerning our true nature cannot be answered dogmatically. It cannot be answered from "outside" by someone else telling us what to believe or not to believe. The answer arises only from a most intimate experience in the depths of our own being. We must struggle to discover who we truly are. The answer does not seem to come easily, and we are lulled into complacency, and even indifference toward the question, by much that today's culture brings our way.

This soporific condition in which we find ourselves was recognized by Vincent van Gogh, who wrote in a letter to his brother Theo: "The large majority of people are asleep and do not wish to wake up."[2]

The Question of Destiny

An equally sensitive topic is the mystery of our relationship to other human beings. We have particular parents, particular sisters and brothers, and particular friends and loved ones. Are these relationships merely the result of coincidence, or is there meaning to be seen in the tapestry of our interpersonal relationships? Are we brought together with others simply by chance? These questions are worth investigating. Superficially, one might say it is all *karma*. But, when we look into the Sanskrit origin of this word, a far more complex significance arises. The word can be translated as "deed" or "action," as well as "movement," and embodies the sense of "something that is accomplished."

We can readily understand that all human relationships are in constant movement in a most complex manner. We relate to one another by deeds in sympathy or antipathy, in love or hate, in complacency or deep interest in the other. It might also be understandable that something of utmost importance for our lives is accomplished in the process of forming, developing, and ending relationships.

We shall attempt a closer look into the working of destiny in relation to karma. We may meet someone, for example, at a particular moment in life, and a conversation ensues that leads to the immediate feeling that we are merely continuing where we left off. We may have the overwhelming feeling of having known this person previously. In contrast, others may feel like strangers, and we may come to know them only gradually or not at all. Further,

---

2. Quoted in Viviane Forrester, *Van Gogh, ou, L'enterrement dans les bles*, Seuil, Paris, 1983.

we may realize that particular individuals we met in our twenties or thirties, have had deep consequences for the course of our life. In fact, those meetings represent turning points of the greatest significance.

It is interesting to note that the English word *coincidence* means "to fall together," as indeed does the German word *Zufall.* The equivalent in French of "by chance" is *par hasard*, derived from the Hebrew "as God wills it." Such thoughts might lead us to consider that every meeting with another human being has a meaning, that "God wills it," so to speak. That we might not immediately fathom the significance of such meetings does not disprove their importance. Can we conceive of being led to one another at a certain time, at a certain place, to mutually accomplish something?

"Who choreographs our meetings?" This an intriguing question, and from it a number of inner experiences can arise. Looking back over the events of my life, I find two distinct qualities: those events that I consciously made happen and those where I seem to have been guided, and did not act intentionally. We may recall, especially in our youth, being prompted quite suddenly to go on a trip to a distant land and, perhaps, discovering something about ourselves, or meeting someone who later played an important role in our destiny. We might miss a bus or a plane and, later, discover that the consequences are far-reaching. Such an incident can prove to be a "blessing in disguise."

Such considerations can awaken feelings of gratitude for having been led by the higher self into certain situations and meetings with certain people, and can provide a feeling of what karma is. To this can be added a further consideration of *compensation*, of rectifying or making right. Karma enables us to make good the errors and the shortcomings of past lives. For this reason we are brought together again and again with those we have known previously.

We find a telling, poetic testimony in a poem by Goethe, written when he was twenty-six, immediately after his first meeting with Charlotte von Stein, with whom he became deeply connected:

> Tell me, what is Destiny preparing?
> Tell me why we two have drawn so near?
> Aeons since, you were my sister, sharing
> Kin with me, or else my wife most dear.

And later in a letter to his friend, Christoph Martin Wieland, Goethe wrote:

> I cannot explain the significance to me of this woman or her influence over me, except by the theory of reincarnation. Yes, we were once man and wife. Now our knowledge of ourselves is veiled, and lies in the spirit world. I can find no name for us—the past, the future, the All.

Such feelings can be overwhelming, although the real significance of the recognition might not dawn until much later. These experiences belong to the most intimate and subtle weavings of the soul.

We shall see later that Rudolf Steiner indicated there are "laws of karma." That I went to a particular country, visited a particular city, met a particular person—such a series of events bears the stamp of necessity; they could hardly have been avoided. And although karma appears inexorable—indeed, has "iron" laws—it should not be associated with punitive measures. Karma does not punish. We are led together with others in order that we might learn from one another and thus grow in our essential humanity. Karma may be viewed as the benevolent teacher on our path in life.

We shall also discover that we ourselves play a part in the orchestration of events. Our own past deeds create the situations of present events. In a most complex manner, out of our higher selves, we are the creators of our destiny, together with the weaving of hierarchical beings.

These considerations raise the question of freedom. If, indeed, so much is determined by necessity, is there room for a free deed? This question is dealt with in great detail by Rudolf Steiner.

We gradually discover that coincidence is a term used to characterize the coming together of events, the significance of which I have not yet fathomed. But why should I not assume that the riddle might be solved at some time in the future?

Meaning in Life

What is the purpose of life on Earth? This is a question that has exercised the minds of the greatest thinkers throughout the ages. In Abrahamic religions—Judaism, Christianity, and Islam—we find an emphasis on learning to obey what is divinely decreed. Traditionally, we are not intended to question since the pattern of life has already been given.

During the Renaissance of the Christian West, a change of consciousness occurred. In Dante's *Divine Comedy* we find a remarkable fourteenth-century poetic saga of precise consequences in the afterlife of our actions on Earth. The soul's journey is dramatically portrayed as it travels (or is fettered) to the circles of hell and purgatory, and finally attains the vision of paradise under the guidance of Beatrice, the eternal feminine. Such visions, valuable as they are, may not satisfy the modern soul, which is largely alienated from spiritual realities, in its search for meaning in life.

Shakespeare's *Hamlet*, written in 1600 when the bard was thirty-five or thirty-six years of age, presents a dilemma that is closer to our contemporary inner struggle. In the "To be or not to be" soliloquy, sleep and death are addressed. Hamlet ponders whether he should bear the blows of fate or make an end to them by committing suicide. Life has lost all meaning for him and he is plunged into the deepest abyss of despair. But as a last resort he recoils from taking his life with his own hand, because he is uncertain of what awaits him once he has crossed into that country "from whose bourne no traveller returns." He decides it is, therefore, preferable to endure what we have than to risk the flight into the unknown.

By 1600 a new age of consciousness had dawned in the West; there was increasing doubt concerning the true nature of birth and death, and the reality of the divine. Human souls began to feel increasingly alienated, culminating in the materialism of the twentieth century, and an almost total denial of the soul itself.

The question of the life's purpose cannot be answered satisfactorily unless we are clear about the nature of sleeping and waking, of birth and death. Here again the modern, searching soul that has glimpsed the abyss of its own nature will not be satisfied with beliefs passed on dogmatically by others, but will seek answers on a path of *personal* experience.

The path pursued by Rudolf Steiner is best illustrated by a quotation from his preface to the first edition (1894) of his book, *Intuitive Thinking as a Spiritual Path:*

> Truth that comes to us from without always bears about it the stamp of uncertainty. We want to believe only what appears to each of us inwardly as truth.
>
> Only the truth can bring us certainty in the development of our individual powers. These powers are lamed in anyone tormented by doubts.... In a world of riddles, people cannot find a goal for their activity.
>
> We no longer want merely to *believe*; we want to *know*.[3]

Emphasis on the experience of individual knowledge (or recognition) characterizes the need of the searching soul today. With this working hypothesis in mind, let us attempt to provide an overview of the history of ideas concerning reincarnation and karma, and then return to our present situation.

---

3. Rudolf Steiner, *Intuitive Thinking as a Spiritual Path: A Philosophy of Freedom*, Anthroposophic Press, Hudson, NY, 1995, p. 254. This book was previously translated as *The Philosophy of Freedom* and as *The Philosophy of Spiritual Activity.*

2.
Historical Survey of Reincarnation and Karma

The Bhagavad Gita's Origin and Influence

Contemplations of reincarnation and karma are found throughout the Hindu scriptures, most notably in the *Bhagavad Gita*, part of the longest poem in the world, the *Mahabharata*, in which we find the teachings of the god Krishna to his disciple Arjuna. The poetic divine teaching in these scriptures was kept alive orally for hundreds of years before the incarnation of Christ. The first English translation of this Sanskrit classic appeared in 1785 and was received with astonishment by those in the West who had not previously been exposed to such ideas. A Russian translation was published three years later, and the first German edition is dated 1803. Alexander Hamilton, upon returning from India in 1802, was obliged to stay in Paris because of the war; there he taught Sanskrit to Friedrich Schlegel, one of the fathers of German romanticism. In his enthusiasm for the Sanskrit language, Schlegel introduced this great poem in Germany and translated it into Latin.

A comprehensive picture of the extent and sublimity of this sacred poem is not possible here, but three aspects should be noted:

1. The ideas of immortality and rebirth are contained in it.

> It [the atman] is born not, nor does it ever die, nor shall it, after having been brought into being, come not to be hereafter. The unborn, the permanent, the eternal, the ancient, it is slain not when the body is slain.... As a person casting off worn-out clothes takes other new ones, so the embodied one, casting off its worn-out bodies, enters others that are new (II:20, 22)[4]

---

4. *The Song of the Lord: Bhagavadgita*, Edward J. Thomas, trans., Charles E. Tuttle Company, Boston, 1992.

2. The practice of yoga is emphasized for gradually overcoming the temptations and allurements of the world of the senses through strict, meditative exercises that bring about purification and enlightenment.

> Or one is reborn even in a family of wise Yogis; yet such a birth as that in the world is harder to win.
>
> There one acquires the contact with intellect that was had in the former body, and from there one strives further for success, O Child of Kuru.
>
> For by that very former exercise one is carried on, even without one's will; and also, desiring to know Yoga, such a person passes beyond the Brama [manifested] in the word.
>
> But the Yogi who strives with great striving, purified from sin, after successfully passing through many births, thereafter goes the highest way. (VII: 42–45)

Yoga is described as "harmony," and once perfection has been attained, "As a lamp in a windless place flickers not, so is this deemed to be a likeness of the Yogi of restrained mind, who practices Yoga of the self" (VI: 19)

3. In the eighteenth book of the *Bhagavad Gita*, the four castes are described. Each soul is born within one of them.

> Calm, restraint, austerity, purity, patience, and uprightness, knowledge, understanding, and belief are the action of the brahmin, arising from their own nature.
>
> Heroism, splendor, firmness, skill, not fleeing in battle, alms giving, and the character of a ruler are the action of the kshatriya, arising from their own nature.
>
> Farming, cattle-keeping, and trade are the action of the vaisya, arising from their own nature; and service is the action of the sudra, arising from their own nature.
>
> By being satisfied with one's proper action, one wins success. (XVIII: 42–45)

It should be noted that the life within each of the castes was strictly regulated; for example, intermarriage between them was strictly forbidden. In other words, laws of karma required that one achieve the task imposed, with the hope that in some future embodiment one might be thought worthy to move to a higher caste. This process in itself might take many lifetimes. Clearly, this social structure arose from a consciousness totally different from the modern Western attitude.

Nevertheless, the influence of the *Bhagavad Gita* on Western minds must be emphasized. The first two aspects especially inspired countless writers, including Henry David Thoreau, Ralph Waldo Emerson, the German and English Romantics, and many others in our own time.

We shall consider later the importance of the appearance of the *Bhagavad Gita* at the turn of the eighteenth and nineteenth centuries when, in addition to the American Revolution, three great revolutions were being enacted in Europe: the French Revolution and its aftermath, which strove for political equality; the Industrial Revolution, which began in Great Britain and struggled with the idea of fraternity; and in Middle Europe the ideal of freedom, championed by the great German idealists Fichte, Schelling, and Hegel, as well as by Goethe, Schiller, Beethoven, and those men and women who gave birth to the Romantic Movement.

Indian Buddhism

The lofty teachings of the Buddha are well known. In the "Sangiti Sutra" the Buddha spoke of four modes of birth, each a result of the measure of awareness achieved by a person in his or her previous life on Earth:

> Brethren, in this world, one comes into existence in the mother's womb without knowing, stays in it without knowing, and comes out from the mother's womb without knowing; this is the first.

> Brethren, one comes into existence in the mother's womb knowingly, stays in it without knowing, and comes out from it without knowing, this is the second.
>
> Brethren, one comes into existence in the mother's womb knowingly, stays in it knowingly, and comes out from it without knowing; this is the third.
>
> Brethren, in this world, one comes into existence in the mother's womb knowingly, stays in it knowingly, and comes out from it knowingly; this is the fourth.[5]

In Sanskrit the word *buddha* signifies one who is enlightened about the meaning of life and death. Gautama Buddha lived in India around 500 B.C., and according to *Mahayana* traditions he taught that a number of bodhisatvas appear at various times during the development of humanity until, having accomplished their task, they attain buddhahood and no longer need to reincarnate.

The teachings of Gautama Buddha encompass a path of purification by which the soul frees itself gradually from the trials and tribulations of the world of the senses until the highest level of consciousness is attained. Here again, laws of karma and reincarnation are clearly stated.

Buddhism rapidly spread from India into Southeast Asia and into Tibet, China, and later Japan, and it found many millions of adherents along the way. In the course of time, the original teachings received important variations.

Other Pre-Christian Aspects

Lao-tze, a Chinese contemporary of Confucius, brought to light teachings of karma and reincarnation from ancient Taoist teachings.

Similar teachings appear in the celebrated Egyptian *Book of the Dead* and Egyptian hermetic works.

---

5. *Dialogues of Buddha (Digha-Nikaya),* Pali Text Society, London, 1971.

Jewish traditions as described in the *Jewish Wars* by Flavius Josephus mention reincarnation quite directly. There are many references to re-embodiment in the books of the secret doctrine of the Kabala. It is interesting to note that these writings deeply influenced Pico della Mirandola, the Italian Renaissance Neoplatonic humanist, as well as John Milton and William Blake who were ardent students of the Kabala.

We cannot turn to the Christian views of reincarnation without first mentioning the remarkable contributions to our subject by Socrates (469–399 B.C.) and Plato (427–347 B.C.). For some fifty years Plato taught at the academy in Athens that bears his name, and some of his teachings flourished relatively uninterrupted for almost a thousand years, until the academy was abolished by Justinian in the sixth century.

In several Platonic dialogues the ideas of pre-existence and re-embodiment play a central part. In the *Meno*, and particularly in the *Phaedrus*, the soul is pictured as a charioteer who drives a pair of winged steeds, one being "noble and good, and of good stock, while the other has the opposite character, and his stock is opposite."[6] Here we find expressed how "the soul, since it is immortal and has been born many times ... has learned everything, so that when someone has recalled a single piece of knowledge—*learned* it, in ordinary language—there is no reason why such a person should not find out all the rest ... for seeking and learning are in fact nothing but recollection."[7]

Important passages delineating the workings of destiny may also be found in Plato's *Laws*. However, the most telling passage is found in the closing lines of *The Republic*, which concludes by mentioning re-embodiment, couched in the "Myth of Er." A tale is told of a brave man who was killed in battle and who, on the twelfth day after his death, lay on the funeral pyre; yet he came to

---

6. *Phaedrus*, 246b (all Plato quotations from *The Collected Dialogues of Plato*, E. Hamilton and H. Cairns, eds., Princeton University Press, 1973).
7. *Meno*, 81d.

life again, and then proceeded to describe what he had seen in the other world:

> . . . those that arrived from time to time appeared to have come as it were from a long journey . . . and those that came from the earth questioned the others about conditions up yonder, and those from heaven asked how it fared with those others. And they told their stories to one another, the one lamenting and wailing as they recalled how many and how dreadful things they had suffered and seen in their journey beneath the earth—it lasted a thousand years—while those from heaven related their delights and visions of a beauty beyond words.[8]

Those souls about to enter earthly life were addressed as follows:

> "Souls that live for a day, now is the beginning of another cycle of mortal generation, where birth is the beacon of death. No divinity shall cast lots for you, but you shall choose your own deity." ... [And] it was a sight worth seeing to observe how the several souls selected their lives ... it was a strange, pitiful, and ridiculous spectacle, as the choice was determined for the most part by the habits of their former lives.... And it fell out that the soul of Odysseus drew the last lot of all and came to make its choice, and, from memory of its former toils having flung away ambition, went about for a long time in quest of the life of an ordinary citizen who minded his own business, and with difficulty found it lying in some corner disregarded by the others, and upon seeing it said that it would have done the same had it drawn the first lot, and chose it gladly.... And after it had passed through that, when the others also had passed, they all journeyed to the Plain of Oblivion, through a terrible and stifling heat, for it was bare of trees and all plants, and there they camped at eventide by the River of Forgetfulness, whose waters no vessel can contain. They were all required to drink a measure of the water, and those who

---

8. *Republic*, 614e.

> were not saved by their good sense drank more than the measure, and each one as he drank forgot all things. And after they had fallen asleep and it was the middle of the night, there was a sound of thunder and a quaking of the earth, and they were suddenly wafted thence, one this way, one that, upward to their birth like shooting stars. Er himself, he said, was not allowed to drink of the water, yet how and in what way he returned to the body he said he did not know, but suddenly recovering his sight he saw himself at dawn lying on the funeral pyre.[9]

In this grand imagination, we see how the soul of Er is allowed to gaze into the mysteries of life before birth and after death. One might suggest that he was initiated into these mysteries and was thus able to bring to humankind images of the other world and yet also find his way into the same body again in order to continue his destiny on Earth.

We are very much reminded here of Egyptian initiation rites as they were practiced for thousands of years. After successfully enduring certain trials, the neophyte was placed into an open sarcophagus and, through ritual words uttered by the presiding priest, into a three-day, death-like state. After this the neophyte was recalled to life and, having experienced the fullness of the spiritual world, attained initiation.

Platonic ideas of human nature and of life and death have permeated the Western world for more than two thousand years. A special flowering can be seen clearly in the Platonic School in Florence, founded at the end of the fifteenth century by Cosimo di Medici, one of the most enlightened men of the Renaissance. Some of the finest minds, such as Marcello Ficino and Pico della Mirandola, came together there to further Platonism and spread Platonic ideas across the whole of Europe. Michelangelo was a pupil of this school in his younger years, and was no doubt deeply influenced by these teachings.

---

9. *Republic*, 617e; 619e; 620c,d; 621a,b.

Biblical Sources

Whether Christ Jesus adhered to the ideas of karma and reincarnation has been much discussed. Some say that these convictions were so widespread in the consciousness of those around Christ Jesus that there was no need to speak about them. We find an explicit affirmation of rebirth in Matthew 11:7, 10–11, and 14–15, a clear statement about the reincarnation of John the Baptist:

> As they went away, Jesus began to speak to the crowds about John: ...This is the one about whom it is written, "See, I am sending my messenger ahead of you, who will prepare your way before you ... and if you are willing to accept it, he is Elijah who is to come. Let anyone with ears listen![10]

This statement is there in the Gospel for all to read, and yet we overlook it, or consider it a metaphor, or minimize it because there are not many references to reincarnation to substantiate it. While some have "ears to hear," others are unable to hear or accept.

In the writings of the early Church Fathers and Christian Gnostics, we find, apart from certain differences in detail, certain statements suggesting ideas of pre-existence and reincarnation. A few should be mentioned by name: Justin Martyr (100–165), Clement of Alexandria (150–215), Tertullian (155–220); and, perhaps the greatest of all, Origen (185–254), whose doctrine of the pre-existence of the soul was declared anathema by the Council of 533, and Emperor Justinian (483–565), who ruled over the whole Eastern Empire, and declared war against the followers of Origen. After that, numerous councils rejected the doctrines of early Church Fathers. Those who held such views were persecuted.

Among the Gnostics in the second century were Basilides, Valentinus, and Marcion. The official Church labeled much of the

---

10. *The Holy Bible: New Revised Standard Version*, Division of Christian Education of the National Council of the Churches of Christ, Iowa Falls, 1989. This edition is used for New Testament quotations throughout this introduction.

broader approaches to Christianity as "Gnostic," and as a result that term came to have a negative connotation. However, those early Christians generally referred to homogeneously as "Gnostics" held a wide range of views and approaches to Christ's teaching. The word *gnostic* comes from the Greek *gnosis*, meaning "to know spiritually," and therefore we cannot assume that the use of the word refers to any specific doctrine or sect. After Constantine, who declared Christianity to be the state religion, esoteric aspects of Christian teachings were carefully exterminated over a relatively short period of time.[11]

The doctrines of pre-existence and reincarnation were kept alive by various heretical streams such as the Manicheans, the Cathars, the Albigensians, and the Bogomils, who spread their powerful influence right through the Middle Ages, lending inspiration to the troubadours of the south of France and various Grail sagas.

One of the darkest chapters in the history of the Dominican Order tells of their appalling success in persecuting and slaughtering the Cathars in southern France for their beliefs. Clearly, the Catholic Church, and later the Protestants, did everything in their power to remove ideas of pre-existence of the soul and reincarnation from Christian doctrine.

Renaissance in the West

We have already mentioned the Neoplatonic scholars that gathered in Florence. In some of their writings they adhered strongly to ideas of reincarnation. Pico della Mirandola clearly stated in his oration *On The Dignity of Man* that "the soul passes out of one body and enters another." The influences of the Platonic Academy marked a major contribution to the advancement of the arts and sciences, and rapidly spread to France, England, and Germany.

---

11. See Andrew Welburn's *The Beginnings of Christianity: Essene mystery, Gnostic revelation and Christian vision*, Floris Books, Edinburgh, 1991. See also by the same author: *Gnosis: The Mysteries and Christianity: An Anthology of Essene, Gnostic and Christian Writings*, Floris Books, Edinburgh, 1994.

Perhaps the clearest expression of the relationship of the human being both to the Earth and to the celestial worlds is found in the writings of Paracelsus (1493–1541), a physician and alchemist, active during his somewhat short life in various parts of Europe. *The Life of Philippus Theophrastus Bombast of Hohenheim (Known as Paracelsus)* by Franz Hartmann contains the following revealing passage:

> Some children are born from heaven, and others are born from hell, because each human being has inherent tendencies, and such tendencies belong to one's spirit, and indicate one's state of existence before birth. Witches and sorcerers are not made at once; they are born with powers for evil. The body is only an instrument: if you seek someone in a dead body, you are seeking in vain.... The form may be destroyed, but the spirit remains and lives, for it is the subjective life.... The body that we receive from our parents ... has no spiritual powers, for wisdom and virtue, faith, hope, and charity do not grow from the Earth. These powers are not the products of physical organization but the attributes of another invisible and glorified body, whose germs are laid within the human being. The physical body changes and dies, the glorified body is eternal. This does not draw nutriment from the Earth but from the eternal invisible source from which one originates.... The temporal body is the house of the Eternal, and we should therefore take care of it, because those who destroy the temporal body destroy the house of the Eternal, and, though invisible, nevertheless the eternal being exists, and will become visible in time.[12]

This passage by Paracelsus has far-reaching implications. Not only is it an eloquent summary of profound esoteric traditions that have continued to weave like a golden thread from ages immemorial, but

12. Franz Hartmann, M.D., *The Life of Philippus Theophrastus Bombast (Known as Paracelsus)*, Kegan Paul, London, (n.d.).

in language that is crisp and precise, points to a new consciousness that will arise in the future when human beings will have developed new capacities by which they will be able to perceive the supersensible. Paracelsus was a man of obvious spiritual stature, and it is certainly no coincidence that his views are gaining considerable interest in our own time.

To quote other great writers and scholars who acknowledged the reality of reincarnation would go beyond the framework of this overview. We can, however, mention Edmund Spenser, Shakespeare (who was clearly aware of Neoplatonic writings), John Donne, and above all the Cambridge Platonists of the seventeenth century.

The Age of Enlightenment

A most striking recognition of reincarnation is the famous epitaph of Benjamin Franklin, which he wrote at the age of twenty-two, and, being a printer, distributed to his many friends:

The Body of B. Franklin,
Printer,
Like the Cover of an Old Book,
Its contents Torn Out
And
Stripped of its Lettering and Gilding,
Lies Here
Food for Worms,
But the Work shall not be Lost,
For it Will as He Believed
Appear Once More
In a New and more Elegant Edition
Revised and Corrected
By the Author.[13]

---

13. *Benjamin Franklin*, Viking, New York, 1952, p. 123.

This was not merely a youthful idea for Franklin, for in a letter to George Whateley dated May 23, 1785, and written when he was seventy-nine, we find the following:

> When I see nothing annihilated and not a drop of water wasted, I cannot suspect the annihilation of souls, or believe that [God] will suffer the daily waste of millions of minds ready made that now exist, and put Himself to the continual trouble of making new ones. Thus, finding myself to exist in the world, I believe I shall, in some shape or other, always exist; and, with all the inconveniences human life is liable to, I shall not object to a new edition of mine, hoping, however, that the errata of the last may be corrected.[14]

These words express profound implications with a delightful lightness typical of Benjamin Franklin's wise contributions to humanity. These statements may be considered as an independent expression of a great Western soul who had struggled from his youth with the profoundest ideas of life and death. What is remarkable is the matter-of-fact, tongue-in-cheek wording of the epitaph, which, nevertheless, because of its directness, provides much food for thought. He compares the physical body to the Book of Life, for instance, in which the events between birth and death are clearly written, followed by death and decay of the outer trappings. His reference to "the work" not being lost obviously refers to the soul that continues to exist, and the I AM that will create, out of what has been experienced, a new capacity and the possibility of "revision and correction by the author." This indicates in a wonderful way that we ourselves are the creators of our own future.

At the same time as the writing and dissemination of the epitaph, the young Franklin began a strict accounting of his daily behavior.

---

14. Leonard W. Labaree, ed., *The Papers of Benjamin Franklin*, Yale University Press, New Haven.

This fact is important, for it shows that he recognized that karma and reincarnation are closely linked with self-development through remembrance and attention to the quality of one's actions, and that this is done entirely out of his own inner forces rather than through the mediation of a priest or spiritual guide. Franklin's epitaph signaled a new consciousness for humankind.

We find a philosophical argument concerning re-embodiment in a booklet by the German dramatist and philosopher, Gotthold Lessing, entitled *The Education of the Human Race*, completed in 1780. In spite of the vastness of the title, the work consists of only one hundred crisp paragraphs covering twenty-four pages. Lessing's argument might be summarized as follows, sounding the central note in the very first paragraph: "That which education is to the Individual, revelation is to the Race." The whole of humanity is being educated through the various cultures and civilizations in the course of time, and we can compare this to the education of the individual. Each age has its own particular gesture. In pre-Christian times we had to learn the importance of obedience. After the coming of Christ, we were educated through imitation. But in Lessing's time, on the eve of the French Revolution and the rise of the Romantic Movement, a new challenge was presented—the task of freedom.

Lessing asks: Is it true that some students learn more quickly than others and cannot acquire full knowledge and ability during a single life; is it unreasonable to consider that we may need to return several times in order to realize our greatest potential?

> But why should every individual human being not have existed more than once upon this world? Is this hypothesis so laughable merely because it is the oldest? . . . Why should I not come back as often as I am capable of acquiring fresh knowledge, fresh expertise? Do I bring away so much from just once that there is nothing to repay the trouble of coming back?
>
> Is this a reason against it? Or, because I forget that I have been here already? Happy is it for me that I do forget. The

> recollection of my former condition would permit me to make only a bad use of the present.
>
> And that which I must forget even now, is that necessarily forgotten for ever?
>
> Or is it a reason against the hypotheses that so much time would have been lost to me? Lost? And how much then should I miss? Is not a whole Eternity mine?[15]

Lessing's contribution is of particular interest because, like Franklin, he arrived at his conclusions by way of a question and answer method, of carefully argued points completely in harmony with the Age of Reason in which he lived.

The Romantic Movement

When he first met Frau von Stein, Goethe was overwhelmed by the feeling that he had known her in a previous life. His deep conviction of repeated lives was also expressed in a poetic form when he compared the soul of man to the water cycle:

> The human soul is like to water;
> From Heaven it cometh
> To Heaven it riseth
> And then returneth to Earth,
> Forever alternating.[16]

Many similar testimonies reflecting deep conviction can be found in the works of William Blake, Friedrich Schiller, William Wordsworth, Sir Walter Scott, Samuel T. Coleridge, Percy Bysshe Shelley, Herman Melville, Gustave Flaubert, Feodor Dostoevsky, Leo Tolstoy, and Henrik Ibsen. For example, in this passage

---

15. D. Alfred Bertholet, *Transmigration of Souls*, Harper & Brothers, New York, 1909, p. 105.
16. *Vermischte Schriften (Miscellaneous Writings).*

Wordsworth addresses an infant:

> Oh, sweet new-comer to the changeful earth,
> If, as some darkling seers have boldly guessed,
> Thou hadst a being and a human birth,
> And wert erewhile by human parents blessed,
> Long, long before thy present mother pressed
> Thee, helpless stranger, to her fostering breast.[17]

also agreed with those who were deeply convinced of ideas about reincarnation.

Two passages from the works of Ralph Waldo Emerson clearly express a belief in reincarnation. It should be borne in mind that, like Thoreau, Emerson was familiar with the *Bhagavad Gita*, which perhaps influenced his thinking on the matter:

> It is the secret of the world that all things subsist and do not die, but only retire a little from sight and afterwards return again.... Nothing is dead; men feign themselves dead, and endure mock funerals and mournful obituaries, and there they stand looking out of the window, sound and well, in some new strange disguise. Jesus is not dead; he is very well alive; nor John, nor Paul, nor Mahomet, nor Aristotle; at times we believe we have seen them all, and could easily tell the names under which they go.
>
> *(Nominalist and Realist)*

> Where do we find ourselves? In a series of which we do not know the extremes, and believe that it has none. We wake and find ourselves on a stair; there are other stairs below us which we seem to have ascended; there are stairs above us, many a one, which go upward and out of sight. But the Genius which according to the old belief stands at the door by which we enter,

---

17. In a 1927 issue of the *Spectator*, London—from a manuscript (sold at Sotheby's) in the hand of his sister Dorothy Wordsworth.

and gives us the lethe to drink, that we may tell no tales, mixed the cup too strongly, and we cannot shake off the lethargy now at noonday. Sleep lingers all our lifetime about our eyes.[18]

(Experience)

Thoreau made a significant contribution to the subject of rebirth. In *Walden* he wrote that he bathed his "intellect in the stupendous and cosmological philosophy of the *Bhagavad Gita* — in comparison with which our modern world and its literature seem puny and trivial."[19] In a later chapter, he wrote, "I am conscious of the presence and the criticism of a part of me, which, as it were, is not a part of me, but spectator, sharing no experience but taking note of it and that is no more I than it is you. When the play, it may be a tragedy, of life is over, the spectator goes his way. It was a kind of fiction, a work of the imagination only, as far as he was concerned." This is a most telling passage, for it shows that Thoreau was endowed with a consciousness soul, the faculty that Rudolf Steiner describes as belonging to the modern mind, an ability to see oneself from the outside as a spectator or stranger. In other words, Thoreau was able not only to live into the events with great sensitivity but also to stand outside them and view himself as from a distance.

In Thoreau's letters we find the following statements, not about any philosophical views that he may have had about reincarnation, but as the expression of certain events in former lives that he was able to recall with precision.[20] On July 8, 1843, he wrote to Emerson: "And Hawthorne, too, I remember as one with whom I sauntered in old heroic times along the banks of the Scamander amid the ruins of chariots and heroes." On April 3, 1850, he wrote to Harrison Blake: "I lived in Judea eighteen hundred years ago, but I never knew that there was such a one as Christ among

---

18. Ralph Waldo Emerson, *The Complete Writings of Ralph Waldo Emerson*, Wise, New York, 1929.
19. Henry David Thoreau, *Walden and Other Writings,* Bantam, NY, 1983.
20. Henry David Thoreau, *The Correspondence of Henry David Thoreau*, Bode and White, ed., Greenwood Press, Westport, CT, 1974.

my contemporaries." On February 27, 1853, again writing to Blake: "As the stars looked to me when I was a shepherd in Assyria, they look to me now a New Englander." And in one of the journals, we find the following, dated July 16, 1851: "As far back as I can remember I have unconsciously referred to the experiences of a previous state of existence."

One might wonder why there is no mention of matters relating to reincarnation in the published body of Thoreau's works. These ideas were simply not acceptable; only now, more than one hundred years later, can the depth of Thoreau's experiences begin to be rightly estimated.

Richard Wagner clearly expressed in letters his beliefs in reincarnation and karma. He had even embarked upon the composition of the musical drama, *Die Sieger* (*The Victors*), with reincarnation as its main theme. Despite having sketched the story in some detail, he decided against completing the work.

In his last mystery opera, *Parsifal*, with its deeply Christian background, Wagner takes us a step further. In the first act, Gurnemanz, Parsifal's teacher, reveals that in a previous life Kundry, a woman endowed with magical gifts, was incarnated as Herodias. Kundry, now in the service of Klingsor, the black magician, had been in her previous life, the wife of Herod and the mother of Salome. After Salome performs the dance of the Seven Veils before the assembled court, Herod, in a moment of exultation, promises to grant her whatever she wishes. Salome then consults her mother, Herodias, who tells her to ask for the head of John the Baptist on a platter. Although Herod is horrified, in order not to lose face in his court, he acquiesces and John the Baptist is beheaded. Later, Herodias waits on the Via Dolorosa in Jerusalem, and as Christ Jesus passes by, carrying his cross, she jeers and mocks him. With infinite love, He meets her eyes. Kundry longs to serve the Grail, but is still fettered to the evil issuing from the dark forces of Klingsor. One can feel that in writing this motif, Wagner was strongly moved by a profound inspiration that revealed the specific workings of karma and reincarnation in the life of a particular human being.

In conclusion, we quote the sensitive poem by the pre-Raphaelite painter and poet Dante Gabriel Rossetti:

> I have been here before.
> But when or how I cannot tell;
> I know the grass beyond the door,
> The sweet keen smell,
> The sighing sound, the lights around the shore.
> You have been mine before. —
> How long ago I may not know:
> But just when at that swallow's soar
> Your neck turned so.
> Some veil did fall. —I knew it all of yore.[21]

The remembrances offered by these authors were clearly born of a deeply felt relationship to the mysteries of karma and reincarnation. Their words can be looked upon as "inklings" arising from the soul, often in a poetic way, and not necessarily experienced by having crossed the threshold of the spiritual world in a clear and conscious manner.

---

21. Dante Gabriel Rossetti, *Collected Works*, vol. 2, Reprint Services, Irvine, CA, 1992.

3.

Rudolf Steiner's Original Contributions

One of the themes recurring in Rudolf Steiner's writings and lectures is that the human consciousness has gone through marked stages of evolution. The way modern human beings think, feel, and act is different in quality from, let us say, the ancient Egyptians. It is not merely a question of a different environment but of a profound difference in cognizing the world.

Briefly, Steiner points to the ancient Egyptians and the Hebrew people as having lived out of what he calls the *sentient soul*, or the feeling life. This period was followed by that of the ancient Greeks, when the individual lived between the inner qualities of the heart and the head through what Steiner calls the intellectual or *mind soul.*

Our modern consciousness dawned at the beginning of the fifteenth century when the *consciousness soul*, as Steiner termed it, began to emerge. During this period, which will continue for another 1,600 years, it is the task of humanity to take hold of the will and find a new relationship to our physical surroundings in order to regain awareness of the spiritual.

Each of these soul periods of humanity encompasses 2,160 years. They may be dated as follows:

Beginning of ancient Egyptian period — 2907 B.C.
Beginning of ancient Greek period — 747 B.C.
Beginning of Modern Age — A.D. 1413

The ancient Egyptian period is preceded by an ancient Persian period, in turn preceded by an ancient Indian period; both of these periods precede historical records. A rich and varied spirituality, mainly of an instinctive quality, permeated the souls of most of humanity up to the beginning of the Egyptian period in 2907 B.C.

The ancient instinctive spirituality may be described as a natural clairvoyance that related human beings to the forces of nature. They still experienced the world around them as alive, and the boundaries between waking and sleeping were not entirely distinct. The ancient Hindu, for example, could still say out of personal experience, "*Tat twam asi*," or "You are that"—that is, that manifestation of Brahman, The Absolute. Communion between self and reality was natural and immediate.

Around 3101 B.C., within the several centuries before the ancient Egyptian period began, a time of spiritual darkness gradually began. This Dark Age, known in Asian esotericism as *Kali Yuga*, lasted for a period of 5,000 years, and came to an end in A.D. 1899.

During this gradual darkening of humanity's consciousness of the spiritual world, a new phase began in our life on Earth, in which humanity was directed more fully into the senses and the physical world. As a result, the soul could no longer maintain an active relationship with the supersensible. In this gradual process, our experience of waking and sleeping, of life and death, went through major transformations. Our relationship to God and the hierarchies—angels, archangels, archai, and so on—came into serious doubt. From our present perspective we can see clearly that, from the beginning of the fifteenth century onward, there was a waning of belief in the reality of the spirit, and simultaneously, a stronger experience of the physical world through the senses. It resulted in the scientific age and a greater involvement in the material world.

The turning point in 1899, at the end of the 5,000-year dark age, marked the beginning of what Rudolf Steiner refers to as the *Light Age*. It was around this time that Steiner began his contribution to human evolution.

Specific Contributions

Rudolf Steiner was thirty-eight at the beginning of the Light Age, and in a remarkable way, had prepared himself through studies in the sciences and humanities to meet the challenge of the New Age of consciousness. A few years earlier his studies had led to a doctoral thesis in philosophy.[22] Steiner developed his ability as a clairvoyant in a methodical and scientific way, and the world of the spirit was as perceptible to him as the physical world is to physical senses.

From the turn of the century until his death in 1925, Rudolf Steiner, apart from elucidating many other disciplines, introduced new dimensions to the mysteries of karma and reincarnation. He pursued these themes for a quarter of a century in his many writings and numerous lecture cycles in many parts of Europe. He primarily addressed the Western consciousness, schooled in the modern materialistic views and generally no longer able to recognize the world of spirit as a reality. His approach could be characterized as one in which clear, free, spiritual thinking is applied to every aspect of life. His approach does not elicit beliefs, but leads rather to individual experience. The question might be formulated: How can we, through a series of hypotheses, arrive at the reality of destiny and re-embodiment through an understanding and experience of the supersensible?

The Threefold Nature of the Human Being

Basic to an understanding of the concept of repeated Earth lives is the threefold nature of the human being: human beings consist of a body, a soul, and a spirit (Self or I). The physical body is subject to birth and death. Its nature is transient. It arises at birth out of the four elements, and at death the corpse is given over to the elements, put aside like an old garment, and eventually, nothing of it will remain.

The I is part of the spiritual world and is immortal. It existed before we were born and lives on after death. It is the *I AM* that we meet in ourselves and in others, and that gives a unique character to each and every human individuality.

---

22. *Truth and Knowledge: Introduction to "Philosophy of Spiritual Activity,"* Steinerbooks, Bauvelt, NY, 1981.

The soul is the mediator between the mortal and the immortal, between the transient and the eternal part of our being, between the body and the spirit. The soul is the inner stage upon which the development of the human being is enacted. For instance, the experiences and happenings of the day are digested by the soul. Wishes, intentions, and ideals that have their source in the spirit also pass through the soul before leading to action in everyday life. On the one hand, the soul responds to outer stimuli, while on the other, it is receptive to the inner inspiration of the spirit, the I AM. Body and spirit meet in the soul, which is the bearer of our destiny and karma. While the body is subject to growth and decay, the law of reincarnation governs the spirit, unless we come to a clear and living concept of the supersensible world—as real as the physical world beheld through the senses—the doctrine of reincarnation can have little meaning for the Western mind.

Our physical body may be looked upon as a vessel, an instrument, or better still, a temple for the spirit. It arises through procreation and the confluence of father and mother. Each of us is subject to the forces of heredity, and it determines many of our traits, such as physical features, race, disposition, and so on. Goethe was particularly clear regarding the characteristics that he received from father and mother: "From my father I have stature and the serious manner of life, from my mother, a joyous disposition and the love of telling stories."[23] It is equally clear that his genius was not received from either.

We shall, therefore, have to distinguish between the individuality and the personality. The individuality refers to the unique spiritual essence of a human being, including individual genius. The personality is the sum total of all the characteristics that we have as a result of heredity, education, environment, and so on. Something of the individuality shines through the personality, but a large portion of the true being remains hidden. We each carry within us much more

23. Quoted in: Rudolf Steiner, *The Gospel of St. John and It's Relation to the Other Gospels*, Anthroposophic Press, Spring Valley, NY, 1982, pp. 204–205.

than is visible through our words and actions. In fact, the greatness of a human being might be characterized as the extent to which one is able to bring that individual quality, the divine spark, to expression via the personality.

The most individual aspect of a person's life can be found in one's biography. Various biographies may have certain similarities, but they are never identical. The more we interest ourselves in the story of a person's life, the more we may discover how a most wonderful, meaningful, and entirely unique pattern reveals itself from birth through the different phases of life. The architect of that pattern is the I AM, shaping each personality differently and giving each a stamp of its own. By and large, we are not conscious of the I AM, though as a result of spiritual development, we may penetrate its hidden recesses.

The I AM is the bearer of our spiritual biography in that it carries within it the totality of our experiences in former lives on Earth. This I AM, or higher self, knows fully what we have achieved and where we have failed, and is our constant guide through all the trials and tribulations of life.

What we usually refer to loosely as I, self, or ego is the dull reflection of the higher self within our limited soul consciousness. The light of the higher self is dimmed by its sojourn in the material body. We lose consciousness of it and often wrongly assume that the "lower" self represents the totality of our inner being. In an age of materialism and technology, this dulling process is considerable and widespread, a result of dimmed perception and the denial of spirit.

In the case of great individualities, such as Saint Francis of Assisi, Michelangelo, Beethoven, and Abraham Lincoln, an unprejudiced study of their biographies can lead us to a conviction of the working of a higher self within them, beyond what heredity and environment might have contributed. Their greatness consists in the extent to which their eternal, higher self was able to manifest on Earth for the benefit of humanity.

To place the threefold nature of the human being in a larger historical context, we should note that in 869, at a church council in

Constantinople, a majority of church officials agreed that the human being is threefold, consisting of body, soul, and spirit, but should be considered a duality of body and soul, with the soul having certain qualities previously attributed to spirit. This marked the beginning of what might be called a devaluation of the human being. Further attempts to devalue humanity emerged in the nineteenth century through the scientific investigations of Darwin, Feuerbach, and others, which led to the idea that the human being had evolved from the ape. Freud contributed to this theory by seeking to show that the soul, as such, did not exist, and that the body was the source of all emotional and feeling life. By the end of the nineteenth century the devaluation was almost complete. The human being was widely viewed as a higher animal or, as is becoming even more widespread today, was compared to a machine. Nonexistence of the soul and Spirit was assumed.

Rudolf Steiner's contribution might be described as the interweaving of seven strands, by means of which we can freely choose a path of soul for our time that leads to greater insight about the mysteries of life and death.

The Path of Thinking

Rudolf Steiner was the first at the dawning of the Light Age to rediscover and proclaim true human nature in its threefoldness, and to express it in such a way that it can be thought and understood by the Western consciousness, which is steeped in the scientific method.

The first path, that of an *enlivened thinking*, is described in one of Steiner's basic writings, *Theosophy*, which explores the nature of the human being, based on an understanding of its threefold organization.[24] The word *theosophy*, as used here, should be understood to mean "divine wisdom" (*theos* = divine, *sophy* = wisdom). The human being bears influences of the divine within.

---

24. Rudolf Steiner, *Theosophy*, Anthroposophic Press, Hudson, NY, 1994.

"Reincarnation and Karma," a chapter from *Theosophy*, is included in this volume. Along with the selected lectures, it provides a helpful foundation for those who wish to experience the reality of reincarnation and karma through the path of thinking. Through specific exercises and approaches to thinking as *spiritual activity*, the first stages of spiritual development can take place, and lead us to our first inklings—or feeling memories—of previous lives and the ways destiny approaches us through our karma. Our thinking activity is usually ruled by our ordinary passions, instincts, and habits, and we do not actually determine our thinking under such conditions as free individuals. Through exercising our thinking, free of the senses and habits, we can begin to experience a new level of thinking infused with the will and warmth of feeling.

The above considerations make it clear that unless we come to a personal experience of the higher or essential Self, our understanding of reincarnation will be wanting. Rudolf Steiner gave a meditation that can greatly assist a student of spiritual science to gain a lively picture of the Self.

More radiant than the Sun,
Purer than the snow,
Finer than the ether
Is the Self
The spirit in my heart.
This Self am I
I am this Self.[25]

The Path of Feeling

Can we begin to be sensitive to the uniqueness of life situations from the point of view of karma and reincarnation? In other words, can we include in our feelings the possibility of karma and reincarnation? We can if we train ourselves to become more observant of

25. This and other meditations contained in *Guidance in Esoteric Training: From the Esoteric School*, Rudolf Steiner Press, London, 1994.

the details of life. The supersensible reality that lies behind physical phenomenon does not necessarily reveal itself in a dramatic manner. Everything that surrounds us is a sign or symbol of the working of the spirit. Revelation of karma and rebirth depends on our ability to read the script. Every mineral, plant, animal, and human has something to impart to us. For this reason Rudolf Steiner emphasized the importance of devotion on the path of spiritual experience. Unless we learn to see and listen with greater attentiveness and inward participation, little progress can be expected.

We can, by means of a simple exercise, heighten our awareness of the workings of destiny. Before going to sleep, we should picture as accurately as possible in the mind's eye what the next day will bring. For the sake of simplicity it is best to choose an ordinary working day with a planned routine. Having completed what might be termed a "prophetic" picture of the happenings that have not yet occurred, we go to sleep.

The next morning dawns and the day unfolds. Now, if in the evening we recall what has happened during the day, we shall find that some things correspond with the "prophetic" picture we had conjured up the evening before. Yet, we shall also discover that in quite a few instances, events do not tally with the picture we formed the previous night. There can be two reasons for this. Either our picture was incomplete, because we omitted certain events due to our own shortcoming, or we will realize that certain events did in fact occur, which we could *not* have foreseen, despite our efforts to form an accurate picture of expected events.

For example, we met an old friend we had not seen for years at a bus stop. Our eyes fell on a book with an intriguing title on the desk of a colleague. We had a chance conversation with a person, whom we had come to dislike, yet he revealed quite a new facet of his personality. And so on.

If we decide to practice such an exercise repeatedly, we gradually discover that the guiding hand of destiny moves within the unforeseeable happenings of everyday life. Our ordinary consciousness usually touches only the surface of things. To perceive the weaving of destiny, a greater sensitivity is needed. This exercise might be characterized as treading a path of feeling, of learning to sense the mysterious weavings of destiny. Such an exercise should be conducted delicately, and we should avoid jumping to fanciful conclusions. On the other hand, what we notice should not be ignored.

Proceeding further, let us ask ourselves how it is that we are here in this room, in this house, in this country? A moment's reflection will lead us back, possibly across decades, to a connection with a certain person in whom we can clearly recognize the beginning of a series of events that has led up to the present situation. At the time, the connection may have appeared insignificant. The pattern may be very complex, much like a piece of music in which the themes interweave, disappear, recapitulate, and develop further. Yet, the thread of destiny is unmistakable—the present moment was potentially there, decades ago. We have merely been guided—sometimes gently, sometimes harshly—to where we find ourselves. Such reflections can engender a deep feeling of gratitude to the many people in our lives who have contributed to the pattern, and to the spiritual world for wise guidance.

First meetings can also be very telling. When we met a certain person, we may have had the feeling of immediate recognition, as if merely continuing a prior acquaintance from where we left off sometime in the past. Whenever we feel strongly drawn to or repelled by someone, irrespective of what they have done, we may be quite certain that the origin of such a relationship lies in a previous earthly life. What is popularly called "love at first sight" wells up from the depth of our being and is often unrelated to apparent reason, at least to begin with.

Earlier we related an experience so beautifully expressed by Goethe in his poem to Charlotte von Stein. It is interesting to note that Frau von Stein shared Goethe's view on rebirth. She considered life on Earth as a school into which the human spirit enters, coming from its heavenly home. Later in a letter to Christoph Martin Wieland, Goethe was even more specific: "Laden therein with weakness, sin and doubts / Grown in knowledge and purified, it enters again through the gates of death, its spiritual home / And continues in different forms of existence to renew itself!"[26]

Remarks made by children are often indicative of the weavings of destiny and the truth of reincarnation. The eminent archaeologist Heinrich Schliemann, when still a boy had informed his father that when grown he would discover exactly where the city of Troy was situated. Many years later, following the most incredible adventures, he did so. Such powerful awareness on the part of a child may be a strong suggestion that pre-earthly intentions are shining through and illuminating the path of destiny for that individual.

When we easily or casually attribute many events in life to chance or coincidence, it is tantamount to saying we cannot understand why they should have occurred. A feeling for reincarnation and karma, to the extent that we patiently make it our own, gradually replaces what may have been considered coincidence with an earnest search for a meaningful pattern. We should not assume that events in life do not make sense simply because we do not understand them, but that we have not yet acquired sufficient insight to read the script, the open book of life as it presents itself to us.

Two of Steiner's lectures represented here were given in Stuttgart in 1912. The first lecture deals with gaining knowledge of reincarnation and karma through certain exercises.[27] Steiner recommended that in practicing these exercises it is important to begin with a feeling directed toward our own biography.

Steiner gave a series of exercises that, if practiced regularly, will lead us to a deeper experience of reincarnation and karma in relation to our meetings with other people.[28] The following mantram called "Peace Dance," given by Rudolf Steiner during a lecture course, *Eurythmy as Visible Speech*, can be most valuable in gaining a deeper relationship to the mysteries of reincarnation and karma.

---

26. Quoted in the periodical *Lucifer*, London, January 1894.
27. Rudolf Steiner, *Reincarnation and Karma: Two Fundamental Truths of Human Existence*, Anthroposophic Press, Hudson, NY, 1992.
28. Rudolf Steiner, *Karmic Relationships: Esoteric Studies,* vol. 2, Rudolf Steiner Press, London, 1974.

The wishes of the soul are springing,
The deeds of the will wax and grow.
The fruits of life are ripening.

I feel my destiny,
My destiny finds me.
I feel my star,
My star finds me.
I feel my goals in life,
My goals in life are finding me.

My soul and the great World are one.

Life grows more radiant about me,
Life grows more arduous for me,
Grows more abundant within me. [29]

The structure of this meditation is of interest: three lines, then six lines, then one, and the concluding three lines. In the first three lines we find a progression from *wishes* to *deeds* to *fruits* corresponding to *springing*, *thriving*, and *maturing*. This is followed by the development of a *feeling* for one's *destiny*, which flows back into cognition out of the feeling effort. From this arises an important experience: alienation is overcome, for "My soul and the great World are one." This relationship of soul to the world is especially important for our time, the results of which are expressed in the last three lines. This meditative exercise can result in a profound change of everyday life at three different levels through a deepening of our soul nature.

The Path of Willing

Initiation in the ancient mysteries took place within the temples, carefully shielded from the surrounding world. One of the principal characteristics of modern initiation as portrayed by

---

29. Rudolf Steiner, *Verses and Meditations*, Rudolf Steiner Press, Bristol, UK, 1993, p. 113.

Rudolf Steiner indicates that initiation occurs today within everyday life. That which was esoteric (and thus strictly guarded), now needs to be expressed exoterically in the Age of Light, and needs to become accessible to all. This is also true with regard to the laws of karma and reincarnation.

Karma is never just an individual matter, and always plays itself out between people. If we wish to make progress in this realm, we should consider that each person we meet brings something to us, and an open attitude of soul will readily confirm this. Consider what we owe to our parents, our brothers and sisters, teachers, friends, and loved ones. What we are today, at the age of thirty-five or forty, for example, is largely determined by what others have given us, whether as joys or sorrows. When we consider this we should bear in mind that, for the most part, these relationships are the result of complex karma stemming from former incarnations.

A difficult further step is to imagine that whatever befalls us is the result of our own will, though perhaps not in our present incarnation. Can we imagine that, in order to correct certain shortcomings of a former incarnation, our higher self now creates certain obstacles or trials in our present life by way of compensation? We could become sensitive to the fact that many of our deeds are not the result of reasonable consideration. In fact, we can become aware of a higher or better self, beyond our normal reasoning powers, that guides us to this or that decision. This kind of guidance is particularly strong in our lives before the age of thirty-five. For example, "something tells us" to visit a foreign country or to change to a new career; we can sometimes recognize the results as guided by something wiser than our conscious self.

Steiner gives us a striking analogy: Suppose we are walking along a city road lined with houses, and that suddenly a tile from a roof above falls on our shoulder. Even in an example like this, we might imagine that our own higher self climbed on the roof, so to speak, loosened the tile, and threw it down at us. Why? That is an intriguing question, and the answers are worthy of our efforts. An entirely new view of life can come to us through such exercises, and we can begin to see that, from a higher point of view, we are creating our own destiny. This attitude, painful though it may be at first, if developed as a soul mood, can be most helpful for an understanding of the mysteries of life.

Karma may be viewed in the light of compensation, or putting something right in relation to others. It is never cruel, though it may appear rigorous, and seen from a higher perspective, it is also not a punishment, but enables us to acquire greater capacities.

Karma affects not only our personal lives but also our professional activities. The career we pursue and activities in which we are involved are not simply matters of chance. A physician or surgeon bears great responsibility to his or her patients. A diplomat can make a tremendous difference in the affairs of state and international events. A banker or broker can affect the lives of thousands of people. A teacher can change the course of a student's life forever. Every activity we engage in involves an element of compensation.

At the founding of the first Waldorf School in 1919, Rudolf Steiner gave an intensive training course to the first group of teachers. At the end of the second lecture, he made an interesting statement about the karmic relationship between teachers and students:

> ... you can be quite certain that we are not led to meet in this life if there are no preconditions for it. Such external processes are, in fact, always the external expression of something inward, however strange this may seem to an external view of the world. The fact that you are here to teach and educate these children from the Waldorf factory and to do everything necessary in this connection indicates that this group of teachers and this group of children belong together karmically. And you become the right teacher for these children through having in former times developed antipathies towards these children; now you free yourself from these antipathies by educating the thinking of these children. And we must develop sympathies in the right way by bringing about the right development of the will.

> So be very clear about this: You can best penetrate the twofoldness of the human being in the manner attempted in our seminar discussion. But you must endeavor to penetrate all aspects of the human being. Through what we attempted in the seminar you will become a good educator only of the thought life of the children. For their life of will you will be a good educator when you endeavor to surround every individual with sympathy, with real sympathy. These things also belong to education: antipathy that enables us to comprehend, and sympathy that enables us to love. Because we have bodies in which there are centers where sympathy and antipathy meet, this also enters the aspect of social interaction between people that is expressed in educating and teaching. I ask you to think this through and take it into your feelings.[30]

The fact that past relationships affect our present lives in such profound ways should not weigh on us like a burden, but we should be prompted to a positive response that brings joy and fresh effort to our lives. Karma presents us with situations that are predetermined, and to which we are inevitably guided through necessity. However, if we inquire into what causes these life situations, the answer will always be found in ourselves, the results of past lives on Earth. One may object that this leaves little room for freedom. It should be remembered, however, that we ourselves have created the present situation, and our response, whether out of habit or freedom, creates conditions for the future. F. W. Zeylmans van Emmichoven, a physician and close associate of Rudolf Steiner, illustrated human freedom through an analogy:

> We wake up every morning amid the surroundings we left behind the previous night. Suppose we have had a difficult letter to write, and because we are unable to complete it, we decide to leave it until the next morning. We shall find the

30. Rudolf Steiner, *Practical Advice to Teachers*, Rudolf Steiner Press, London, 1988, p. 39.

> letter again next day as we left it; that is inevitable. But we are at liberty to destroy the letter or to write a fresh one, or to delay even further the writing of it. And thus it is in life. What we find, whom we meet, and also in what particular circumstances we find ourselves, for instance, all this is given, but we are free to deal with them to the extent that our capacities allow.[31]

Goethe said in his *Faust* that the gods could redeem only the human being who is always striving. Indeed, in life the quality of striving should be emphasized rather than mere achievement. Freedom, rightly understood, is a growth process that arises out of a striving human soul. Human freedom relies on inner activity.

The all-too-prevalent idea that freedom is the liberty to do whatever one wants is not in accord with the truth of karma and reincarnation. Neither is fatalism, which overstresses necessity. A fatalistic attitude to life's circumstances is a dull response to karma that meets us from the past. Karma presents us with necessity as a constant challenge to improve on what we have already done. Life has a dynamic, evolving quality, as does the I AM, which is active in every human being.

For this reason, self-education should play a central part in the life of every adult. This does not mean the mere accumulation of knowledge and facts, but rightly understood, should lead to the gradual development of virtues and capacities that lie dormant in the soul. This is the true hallmark of freedom.

Benjamin Franklin, as mentioned earlier, began an accounting of his own actions in daily life. In his early twenties, he had discovered thirteen virtues, which he carefully listed and described, and every day he practiced them energetically. In the morning he resolved to do the good, to be courteous, to act modestly. In the evening he assessed the results of his efforts. By means of a careful accounting, he kept a record of his self-imposed educational discipline, placing

---

31. F. W. Zeylmans van Emmichoven, *The Reality in Which We Live,* trans. René Querido, New Knowledge Books, Sussex, 1964.

a mark for the day against the virtues he had failed. To begin with, as he relates himself, the pages were filled almost exclusively with marks, and he recalls that in the process he made many discoveries about himself. But gradually the picture improved as he continued this practice, patiently, over the years.

We can be certain that in addition to self-improvement, such a training of character during this lifetime also has definite results in future incarnations, possibly endowing the personality with quite remarkable capacities with which to serve humanity with deeper insight. Whatever we decide to undertake in the way of spiritual development or self-education is never the result of mere outer compulsion, for it is in the most intimate resolves that true freedom really begins.

It lies within the freedom of the individual to overcome character blemishes such as envy or untruthfulness, and if we ignore these defects, they obviously hamper our present life on Earth. But deeper insight into the laws of karma through the spiritual development shows that moral failings in one incarnation may actually manifest as physical weaknesses or disabilities in the next, and helps us to understand that our own free will breaks the bonds of necessity within karma. The polarity between necessity and freedom is one of the most profound mysteries relating to human existence and the greatest philosophers throughout the ages have wrestled with the implications of this question. In *Intuitive Thinking as a Spiritual Path*, Rudolf Steiner addresses this problem in direct terms that are accessible to anyone prepared to think carefully and deliberately. This work was the first of five fundamental books in which Rudolf Steiner presented to the public the essential ideas of his philosophy and spiritual insight.[32]

---

32. *Intuitive Thinking as a Spiritual Path: A Philosophy of Freedom*; *Theosophy: An Introduction to the Spiritual Processes in Human Life and the Cosmos*; *How to Know Higher Worlds: A Modern Path of Initiation*; *An Outline of Occult Science*; and *Christianity As Mystical Fact*. See bibliography.

With this profound concept of freedom in mind, we can now turn to the following meditation to deepen our understanding of the mysteries of karma and destiny.

> If to the Spirit of the All-World Being
> Thou turn with heart and mind,
> Then wilt thou find thyself:
> Free human being and sovereign player
> In the fields of Fate.
>
> But if thou turn from Him away
> And in vain glory of the hour find distraction,
> Then wilt thou lose thyself:
> Tossed like the empty human figment,
> The toy of Fate.[33]

Life Before Birth and Life After Death

In many of his books and lectures, Rudolf Steiner came to terms with the meaning of karma and reincarnation, which can be understood only when we consider our existence between death and a new birth. Before incarnation, the human being is given an overview of the coming embodiment in which the many threads of destiny are seen. This could be compared to the viewing of an expanse of valley from the top of a mountain. It is wonderful to consider a new born baby, how the whole of its coming life is imprinted and will unfold gradually in the various phases of life, becoming more and more the true and intended individuality. From first learning to walk and speak to becoming conscious of oneself in the world, the whole of our Earthly existence is comprised of a series of complex metamorphoses of movement, feeling, and thinking. In the sixth or seventh year, about the time that a child changes teeth, the

---

33. A private meditation given by Rudolf Steiner in 1920, *Verses and Meditations*, Rudolf Steiner Press, Bristol, UK, 1993, p. 51.

beginning of a greater independence, especially from the mother, can be seen in a child's development. A further degree of individuality and independence can be observed at the time of puberty. Then, around the eighteenth to twenty-first year, the I AM should truly enter into an individual's biography.

Gradually, as adults, we are called on to enter the school of life and respond to the various challenges presented by the complex weaving of destiny, which unfolds in seven-year periods, each having a characteristic quality. Turning-points occur at seven, fourteen, twenty-one, twenty-eight, thirty-five, and so on.[34]

A person who has reflected sufficiently on the cause of a human life can understand the reality of Wordsworth's "Ode: Intimations of Immortality from Recollections of Early Childhood":

> The child is father of the Man
> And I could wish my days to be
> Bound each to each by natural piety.
> . . . . . .
> Our birth is but a sleep and a forgetting:
> The Soul that rises with us, our life's Star,
> Hath had elsewhere its setting,
> And cometh from afar:
> Not in entire forgetfulness,
> And not in utter nakedness,
> But trailing clouds of glory do we come
> From God who is our home:
> Heaven lies about us in our infancy!
> Shades of the prison house begin to close
> Upon the growing Boy.

---

34. The subject of human life phases is explored in Bernard Lievegoed's *Phases: The Spiritual Rhythms of Adult Life*, Rudolf Steiner Press, London, 1993. Also see George & Gisela O'Neil, *The Human Life*, Mercury Press, Spring Valley, NY, 1990, and William Bryant, *The Veiled Pulse of Time*, Lindisfarne Press, Hudson, NY, 1993.

But He beholds the light, and whence it flows,
He sees it in his Joy;
The Youth, who daily farther from the east
Must travel, still is Nature's Priest,
And by the vision splendid
Is on his way attended.
. . . . . .
Hence in a season of calm weather
Though inland far we be,
Our Souls have sight of that immortal sea
Which brought us hither,
Can in a moment travel thither,
And see the Children sport upon the shore,
And hear the mighty waters rolling evermore.[35]

It is not easy in an age of widespread intellectualism and technological growth to appreciate the subtle, sensitive spiritual implications of this poem. It is not merely as a piece of poetic fancy, but an expression of supersensible truths.

Let us reflect for a moment on the imagery. Ancient traditions corroborate the fact with a symbolic image, that before we incarnate we drink the "draft of forgetfulness." As we mature, the reality of the spiritual world that we enjoyed before birth gradually fades away. But "inklings" are often sensed by a child, and the "clouds of glory" with which we come, might well be the talents of our essential self, beyond what we receive through heredity. Indeed, "shades of the prison house begin to close" upon us as we grow, and the spiritual world fades. But the "light of day," what we perceive through our senses, grows stronger.

"Intimations" by the British poet Thomas Traherne (1636–1674) contains some of the most sensitive descriptions of uncommon

35. Quoted in Ernst Lehrs' *Man or Matter: Introduction to a Spiritual Understanding of Nature on the Basis of Goethe's Method of Training, Observation, and Thought*, Rudolf Steiner Press, London, 1985, p. 144.

powers of memory, which he, as a teacher, felt were of great value to him. The following quotation is a poetic pre-birth image:

> Those pure and virgin apprehensions I had from the womb and that divine light wherewith I was born are the best unto this day, wherein I can see the Universe. By the gift of God they attended me into the world, and by His special favor I remember them till now. Verily, they seem the greatest gifts His wisdom could bestow, for without them all other gifts had been dead and vain. They are unattainable by books, and therefore I will teach them by experience.[36]

In the following memory-picture, Traherne speaks of the nature of his soul during his earliest years on earth:

> Certainly Adam in Paradise had not more sweet and curious apprehensions of the world, than I when I was a child.
>
> All appeared new, and strange at first, inexpressibly rare and delightful and beautiful. I was a little stranger, which at my entrance into the world was saluted and surrounded with innumerable joys. My knowledge was Divine. I knew by intuition those things which since my Apostacy I collected again by the highest reason. I was entertained like an Angel with the works of God in their splendor and glory, I say all in the peace of Eden; Heaven and Earth did sing my Creator's praises, and could not make more melody to Adam, than to me. All Time was Eternity, and a perpetual Sabbath. Is it not strange, that an infant should be the heir of the whole world, and see those mysteries which the books of the learned never unfold?[37]

---

36. Thomas Traherne, *Centuries*, Harper & Brothers, New York, 1960, p. 109. Special indebtedness is owed to Dr. Ernst Lehrs, one of the first Waldorf teachers, for having directed my attention to Traherne's writings. More on this remarkable and little known poet can be found in Dr. Lehrs' book.
37. Ibid., pp. 109–110.

The same experience, though in a different form, is sensitively expressed in the opening lines of Traherne's poem, "Wonder." (The original spelling is here preserved.)

> How like an Angel came I down!
> How bright are all things here!
> When first among his Works I did appear
> O how their GLORY did me crown!
> The World resembled his ETERNITIE,
> In which my Soul did Walk;
> And evry Thing that I did see
> Did with me talk.[38]

Such rare and vivid testimonials can help the student of spiritual science, through imagination, to enter more deeply into the mysteries of childhood and prenatal consciousness. The German romantic poet, Novalis, also gave expression to these mysteries: "When we are born, we die to the world of the spirit and when we die, we are born into the spirit."

This theme has evoked considerable interest in the past thirty years, and fascinating accounts of "near-death experiences" have been widely publicized. Such experiences have led souls to powerful insights across the threshold of death, from which they return into everyday life, often deeply transformed.[39]

Rudolf Steiner illuminated the mystery of the soul after death through his ability to see into the spiritual world with depth and accuracy. He described the results of his investigations in many of his books and lectures. According to Steiner, when the physical body is laid aside at death, a grand, expanding panorama is viewed inwardly by the departing soul for a period of about three days.

---

38. Quoted in Ernst Lehrs, *Man or Matter*, pp. 145–149.
39. See, for example, Raymond Moody, *Life after Life*, Mockingbird, Atlanta, 1975; George Ritchie, *Return from Tomorrow*, Fleming Revell, Old Tappan, NJ, 1978; Calvert Roszell, *The Near-Death Experience*, Anthroposophic Press, Hudson, NY, 1992.

During this time the totality of everything that has been experienced in the recently finished life on Earth is displayed in a vivid memory tableau. Everything is presented at one time rather than in the sequence of experiences as they were lived.

It is preferable for the person not to be buried or cremated until such time is past. This is, indeed, the wise practice of the "wake," and loved ones and friends may, during this time, commune with the departed soul by reflecting on common memories. This may help the soul considerably, as may the reading to the dead. One should choose, for instance, enlightened texts from the Bible and other sacred writings, especially those with which the departing soul was familiar, or certain passages from the literature of spiritual science that speak of the soul's journey after death. Rudolf Steiner suggested many readings and meditations that enable us to build a secure bridge between the two worlds. The following meditations were given for this purpose:

I gaze upon thee
In the spiritual World
In which thou art.
May my love mitigate thy warmth,
May my love mitigate thy cold,
May it reach out to thee and help thee
To find thy Way
Through Spirit-darkness
To Spirit-Light

. . . . .

Upward to thee strive the love of my soul,
Upward to thee flow the stream of my love!
    May they sustain thee,
    May they enfold thee
    In heights of Hope,
    In spheres of Love.[40]

---

40. *Verses and Meditations*, pp. 211, 213.

After a three day period, the soul will recall its earthly experiences in reverse order, from death back to birth. In addition, we experience what we have done to others from their points of view. For example, I may have justifiably hurt someone during my life, or I may done it out of irrepressible anger. Now, in this period after death, I will experience that hurt from the point of view of the other—his or her pain, humiliation, feelings of betrayal, and so on. From this process a wish arises to compensate, to put things right, but the body is no longer at our disposal and this desire will have to wait to be integrated into the next incarnation. This "journey-in-reverse" is referred to in Sanskrit as *kamaloka*, and in Christian theology corresponds to purgatory. It is a time of cleansing, of purification, a self-assessment, brought about in cooperation with the spiritual hierarchies. It takes place in what Steiner called the *Moon sphere* and lasts for about a third of the previous life on Earth.

The journey through the planetary spheres—Mercury, Venus, Sun, Mars, Jupiter and Saturn—begins as *kamaloka* ends, but it is beyond the scope of this introduction to recount fully the descriptions provided for us by Rudolf Steiner on this subject.[41] However, the extent to which we remain awake in these different spheres depends on our capacities developed during earthly life through our own efforts. This fact is closely connected to the questions: What do I have that can be returned to the spiritual hierarchies, and what qualities have been incorporated into my I AM that contribute to the evolution of humanity?

The turning point in this period after death occurs at the *Midnight Hour*, when we begin to prepare for our journey into the next incarnation. Depending on our karma, each of the planetary spheres will endow us with certain characteristics. For instance, the future historian will receive the gifts of Saturn, and the sculptor or writer, those of Jupiter.

---

41. Rudolf Steiner, *Life between Death and Rebirth*, Anthroposophic Press, Hudson, NY, 1968. These lectures provide a thorough examination of the concepts introduced here briefly.

Mars endows with strength and the will to transform and revolutionize a particular aspect of life. Musicians, especially composers, receive the great gifts of the Sun. All activities based on beauty and harmony are endowed with the gifts of Venus. Mercury gives its qualities to those who will practice medicine and the healing arts, or be involved in public relations. Secretaries and reporters are likely to receive the gifts of the Moon.

Karma is complex and considers the individual's relationships to family, ethnicity, nation, and the era into which one incarnates in order to balance past actions and build new capacities. A child brings echoes of "clouds of glory" from pre-natal life, and gradually, in the course of life, these many-layered memories are hidden, and only come to expression with the consciousness of I AM. It is quite clear that these considerations require profound, regular study and should not be taken lightly, but if one is prepared to use these ideas as working hypotheses for living, much can be gained, not only for the soul's comfort and understanding, but for genuine knowledge and capacity for the future

Rudolf Steiner's Four Mystery Plays

The Mystery Plays occupy a pivotal role in the work of Rudolf Steiner, not only because they were written and performed at the midpoint of his spiritual work, but also because they marked the beginning of a penetration of his endeavors by the arts. Until then, Anthroposophy had been presented through books and lectures, suffused with a meditative and enlightened thinking element. Now, through a renewal of the arts, a strong feeling element was brought forward.

For four years beginning in 1910, Steiner gathered together in Munich a group of amateur actors who were familiar with his teaching, and each summer they performed his mystery plays in a rented theater. The dramas were accompanied by four lecture cycles, given in order to illuminate the dialogue, music, and eurythmy that comprised the performances.

According to Steiner the first play, *The Portal of Initiation* (1910), leans heavily on an inspiration stemming from Goethe's fairy tale, *The Green Snake and the Beautiful Lily.*[42] The second drama, *The Soul's Probation* (1911), contains Rosicrucian secrets and influences from the Knights Templar and their ordeals during the Middle Ages. Steiner stated that the first two plays were authored by the inspiration of Christian Rosenkreutz, and emphasizes that they were written *through* rather than *by* himself. The other two dramas, *The Guardian of the Threshold* (1912) and the *The Souls' Awakening* (1913), arose mainly out of Anthroposophy and Steiner's own spiritual investigations and are therefore attributed to him as author.[43]

These plays provide a unique and new dimension to the theme of karma and reincarnation. We are introduced to a number of characters seeking a path to the spirit under the guidance of an initiate named Benedictus. These characters are revealed to be karmically connected, but are at very different stages of inner development.

We are introduced to Maria, a remarkable woman who has attained considerable spiritual capacity; Johannes Thomasius, her friend, is a painter who is deeply troubled at times; Strader, the scientist, finds it difficult to accept the reality of a spiritual world; Capesius is a professor of history who is not always able to cope with the world around him; through spiritual vision Theodora proclaims the coming of Christ in the etheric realm, the life body of the Earth. Felix Balde and his wife Felicia live in the country; they are deeply connected with the elemental beings that live and weave together in nature. Throughout the four dramas the characters in this play interact in both the physical and the spiritual realms, with each of them facing particular trials, while we witness their relationships through various incarnations.

---

42. Goethe's fairy tale is contained, with Steiner's first mystery play, in *The Portal of Initiation*, Steinerbooks, Blauvelt, NY, 1981. See also Paul Allen and Joan deRis Allen, *The Time Is At Hand!*, Anthroposophic Press, Hudson, NY, 1995.

43. Rudolf Steiner, *The Four Mystery Plays*, Rudolf Steiner Press, London, 1982. The fourth play also appears in *The Souls' Awakening: Soul and Spiritual Events in Dramatic Scenes*, Anthroposophic Press, Hudson, NY, 1995.

With the help of Theodora, Maria remembers her past during pre-Christian Celtic times and how it connects her with Johannes. Later we are shown the interrelationships of these characters during the Middle Ages, and it gradually becomes clear how occurrences in the past affect the present. In the fourth drama, we are led back to Egyptian times, and the characters increase their awareness and understanding of what they are living through in their current lives. The four dramas take place over a period of about fifteen years, and we witness how the characters develop through their growing knowledge of karma and reincarnation.

These dramas also address the problem of evil. Theater in the Middle Ages represented the devil on the stage as a character affecting the destinies of other characters. The tension between good and evil was directly portrayed and became the central theme of the dramatic plot. *Theophilus* was an early example of this kind of drama, and Christopher Marlowe's *Dr. Faustus* portrayed a strong and dramatic image of evil.

In *Faust*, Goethe's monumental two-part play, Mephistopheles appears constantly at Faust's side, and is the personification of evil. The name *Mephistopheles* comes from the Hebrew *mephiz*, meaning "deceiver" and *topel*, meaning "liar." Rudolf Steiner had the highest regard for Goethe, but pointed out that with *Faust* he could not differentiate clearly between the two aspects of evil. In the staging, however, Faust is accompanied and tempted in the first part of the play by a Mephistopheles dressed in red, which suggests a luciferic being, whereas in part two, Mephistopheles is dressed in black, suggesting a satanic-ahrimanic adversary.

Steiner clearly distinguishes these two forces, and from 1909 onward spoke of their influences in the daily life of humanity. Originally, both Lucifer and Ahriman were high spiritual beings, and fell because they chose to fulfill an opposing role in the development of the cosmos and of humanity. They act as tempters and agents involved in human karma, but each in very different ways. Lucifer constantly seeks to seduce human beings into the supersensible world and away from our earthly tasks. He is the spirit of vanity, pride, ambition, and an overbearing confidence in oneself. He rejects humility, modesty, and any form of moral freedom. Ahriman is the spirit of death and seeks to bind human beings to the material and sense realm. He attempts to blind humanity to the reality of spirit and hinders those who strive for insight into the supersensible world. The human being, to be free, must tread a middle path, and find the golden mean between the seductions and allurements of these two powerful beings. The effects of these two adversaries can continue from incarnation to incarnation. In one life we might be more subject to Lucifer's influence, in the next, circumstances will present us with an ahrimanic challenge, so that we may balance out our experiences. Steiner shows repeatedly how it is Christ that creates and sustains the Middle Way between these two aspects of evil.

Revealing Individual Reincarnations

The first scene in *The Guardian of the Threshold*, Steiner's third play, depicts "the waiting room to the Sanctuary of the Rosicrucian Brotherhood." The prevailing color of the room is blue, and pictures of Elijah, John the Baptist, Raphael, and Novalis are displayed to illustrate four types of initiation, which correlate to changes of human consciousness. In 1912, shortly before this play was written, Rudolf Steiner spoke for the first time about the sequence of these four individualities, stating that they represented four embodiments of the same being. Elijah the prophet is mentioned on numerous occasions in the Old Testament, especially in the Book of Kings. He confronted the priests of Baal, representatives of the evil arts of black magic, by bringing down fire from heaven, and consequently, King Ahab and his wife Jezebel plotted to kill him.

John the Baptist shared Elijah's fiery spirit, and in fact, was the reincarnated prophet. He belonged to an order of Essenes that lived in the desert, and came to baptize the thirty-year-old Jesus of Nazareth so that the Christ would descend into his human body for the period of three years. John the Baptist taught that the Christ would baptize with fire, whereas he could only baptize with water.

Raphael (1483–1520) was profoundly imbued with a healing influence, which can be seen in his many portrayals of the Madonna and Child. What was once outer fire in Elijah and John the Baptist became internalized as the warmth and light that permeate Raphael's art. It was said that whenever Raphael entered a war-torn city (and there were many at this time in Italy), there would be peace for the duration of his stay, and people spoke of his presence as "angelic." Like John the Baptist, he encountered an untimely death.

Of these four individualities, the poet Novalis (1772–1801), also known as Friedrich Philipp von Hardenberg, is the least known today.[44] As a contemporary of Beethoven, Schiller, and Goethe, Novalis was one of the foremost German Romantic writers and poets, though his profession was clerk and mining engineer. The deeply religious poems of Novalis were composed during a period of about five years, following the death of his beloved fifteen year-old fiancee. From the spiritual realm, she became his constant inspiration, and he described the way in which he was able to make this connection after her death. His "Hymns to the Night" and "Spiritual Songs" display a profound and deeply felt purity of soul. Novalis had intended to write a comprehensive philosophical work that would encompass the sciences, arts, and humanities. Novalis died at the age of twenty-nine, and his *Fragments,* the notes and jottings of that intended work, are like seeds, filled with vitality and entering into life's many domains.

Rudolf Steiner spoke of John the Baptist, Raphael, and Novalis on September 28, 1924 in his final public lecture:

> Whatever we have before us in immediate sense-reality, whatever the eye can see and recognize as beautiful—all this, through the magic idealism that lives in the soul of Novalis, appears in his poetry with a well-nigh heavenly splendor....

---

44. Novalis, *Hymns to the Night / Spiritual Songs*, trans. George MacDonald, Temple Lodge Press, London, 1992.

> And so we see in Novalis a radiant and splendid forerunner of the Michael stream ... to prepare the work that will be accomplished at the end of the century, and that will lead humankind past the great crisis in which it is involved.[45]

In the seventh scene of *Portal of Initiation*, the principal characters are in the realm of the spirit. Theodora, through clairvoyance, reveals previous incarnations of Maria and Johannes in Hibernia. This is the first time in Steiner's Mystery Plays that former lives of the characters are mentioned specifically. At the end of the scene, Benedictus appears; his closing words give deep insight into the working of karma:

> You have been joined by destiny
> together to unfold the powers
> which are to serve the good in active work.
> And while you journey on the path of soul,
> wisdom itself will teach you
> that highest goal can be achieved
> when souls will give each other spirit certainty,
> will join themselves in faithfulness
> for healing of the world.
> The spirit's guidance has united you in knowledge;
> so now unite yourselves for spirit work.
> The rulers of this realm bestow on you,
> through me, these words of strength ....

We can see clearly, from a spiritual perspective, what is intended in the lives of human beings joined by karma. Through recognition of the threads of destiny, light-filled purpose is given to the future. Benedictus continues:

---

45. Rudolf Steiner, *The Archangel Michael: His Mission and Ours*, Anthroposophic Press, Hudson, NY, 1995, pp. 282–283. The complete address was published as *The Last Address*, Rudolf Steiner Press, London, 1967.

Light's weaving essence radiates
from person to person
to fill the world with truth.
Love's blessing gives its warmth
to souls through souls
to work and weave the bliss of all the worlds.
And messengers of spirit join
human works of blessing
with purposes of worlds.
And when those who find themselves in others
can join one with the other
the light of spirit radiates through warmth of soul.

Christ as the Lord of Karma

Anthroposophy is deeply rooted in esoteric Christianity, but in a way that elaborates a view of the Cosmic Christ that goes far beyond any concept generally current today. Steiner's book *Christianity as Mystical Fact* raises a fundamental question: How can something be both fact and mystical? Rudolf Steiner shows in this and subsequent lectures that the Christ is a cosmic entity who, at a particular moment in history, brought love and the possibility of salvation to humankind by incarnating on Earth for three years, from the time of Jesus' baptism until the Mystery of Golgotha. The Christ did not enter a child, but descended into Jesus of Nazareth, a rabbi and a carpenter of remarkable wisdom. It was Jesus who, from the time of King David, was intended to become the vehicle of the Christ. A clear distinction is made between the Cosmic Christ and Jesus of Nazareth, yet the two became one—a God-Man—for a period of three years. The *Mystery of Golgotha,* as Steiner termed it, describes the events at the turning point of time—the Death and Resurrection of Christ Jesus. To the degree that the events took place within the physical, perceptible world, facts are described, and mystery is a part of these events through workings of high spiritual beings.

Steiner gradually revealed through spiritual insight that everything is evolving—not just the human being, the kingdoms of nature, and Earth itself, but all the levels of spiritual hierarchies and the cosmos as a whole are going through continual transformation. We should form the imagination that in pre-Christian times the Cosmic Christ dwelled in the spiritual world, inspiring the great ancient religions. He then became man on Earth, appeared in the physical world, went through death, and after the Resurrection, as a spiritual being, united himself with the *etheric body* (life sheath) of the Earth. This is clearly indicated in the Ascension scene described at the beginning of the Acts of the Apostles:

> When he had said this, as they were watching, he was lifted up, and a cloud took him out of their sight. While he was going and they were gazing up toward heaven, suddenly two men in white robes stood by them. They said, "Men of Galilee, why do you stand looking up toward heaven? This Jesus, who has been taken up from you into heaven, will come in the same way as you saw him go into heaven." (1:9–11)

The cloud covering around the Earth in its various formations of water and air provides the life garment of our planet. The Christ disappeared into this living substance and He will reappear again out of it. According to Steiner, the mystery of the Second Coming, will be a spiritual-etheric, not a physical, reappearance of the Christ.

The uniting of the Resurrected One with the etheric body of Earth has been a gradual process spread over many centuries. With the dawn of the Light Age at the beginning of this century, the transformation of the Christ, as well as the consciousness of humanity, makes possible the appearance of the Etheric Christ to an increasing number of human beings, bringing healing, comfort, and guidance.

In *The Portal of Initiation*, Theodora, a seer, proclaims to a gathering of friends the impending appearance of Christ in the etheric. The ability to see this will depend not on faith, but on a newly won, light-filled spiritual vision:

A human being
emerges from glowing light.
It says to me,
You shall proclaim to all
who have the will to hear
that you have seen
what human beings soon will experience.
Christ once lived on Earth,
and from His life it follows
that as soul He embraces
human growth on Earth.
He is united with the spiritual part of Earth,
but human beings cannot yet behold Him
in the form in which He reveals Himself,
because they lack the eyes of spirit
that will be theirs.
Now the time draws near
when with new power of sight
human beings on Earth will be endowed.
What once the senses could behold,
when Christ lived on the Earth,
will be perceived by human souls.

Theodora's speech expresses the essence of the new Christ revelation. This play was written and performed in Munich during the summer of 1910, the same year that Steiner delivered more than twenty lectures on this theme. The theme of the reappearance of Christ has become a cornerstone of esoteric Christianity, and an ever growing number of men and women will experience the Christ as Comforter and Guide, regardless of whether they have been prepared in any special way. The deed of the Second Coming is one that will gradually permeate the whole of humanity. The special task of Anthroposophy is to help men and women to recognize and understand the significance of this experience of Christ.

There is yet another dimension to this mystery. Together with these events, the Christ has taken on another momentous task: He has become the *Lord of Karma.* Before the coming of Christ two thousand years ago, the phrase "an eye for an eye, and a tooth for a tooth" was the predominant guideline for human interaction, and was given by Moses as the Law. Appalling feuds, civil wars and rivalries, and vengeance were all justified by this concept. Moreover, as we look around us today, terrible rivalries and warring factions still perpetrate these horrors on one another, bringing death and misery to millions. Unfortunately, much of humanity still acts on this Mosaic principle that should have been relinquished long ago.

Today, as the New Age is dawning, we can, if we wish, establish our connection with the Christ, who inspires love and forgiveness. Karma continues to operate, constantly bringing balance to our actions. Christ, as Lord of karma, helps those who trespass to develop a new relationship to their own mistakes and shortcomings, and to others they have harmed. This new approach is expressed in an archetypal way in the story of the woman accused of adultery, as related in the Gospel according to Saint John (8:3–11):

> The scribes and the Pharisees brought a woman who had been caught in adultery; and making her stand before all of them, they said to him, "Teacher, this woman was caught in the very act of committing adultery. Now in the law Moses commanded us to stone such women. Now what do you say?" They said this to test him, so that they might have some charge to bring against him.
>
> Jesus bent down and wrote with his finger on the ground. When they kept questioning him, he straightened up and said to them, "Let anyone among you who is without sin be the first to throw a stone at her." And once again he bent down and wrote on the ground. When they heard it, they went away, one by one, beginning with the elders; and Jesus was left alone with the woman standing before him. Jesus straightened up and said to her, "Woman, where are they? Has no one condemned you?"

> She said, "No one, sir." And Jesus said, "Neither do I condemn you. Go your way, and from now on do not sin again."

Christ prevented the scribes from acting according to the Law of Moses; He forgave the woman and told the woman to sin no more. He made a mark on the Earth, indicating that the action committed will have to be compensated for on Earth in a subsequent incarnation. Christ as the Lord of karma does not punish, but gives us the possibility to rectify our deeds through the love and understanding provided by the Cosmic Christ.

We have attempted to consider aspects of necessity and freedom relating to the laws of karma. Karma brings human beings together in a way that is inescapable, but we are increasingly free to act as we will within the circumstances presented by karma. It would indeed be un-Christian to meet someone who has fallen into hard times and say: It's their karma, I should let it take its course and not interfere. Christ Jesus suggested that we can intervene lovingly in the other's destiny, and offer whatever assistance we might be able to give.

Karma is one of the most complex subjects relating to esoteric Christianity in daily life, and we have only been able to give a glimpse of its implications. The cycle of lectures *From Jesus to Christ* provide further insight for the reader interested in pursuing this theme.[46]

In conclusion, I quote a few words that contain the essence of what Rudolf Steiner sought to communicate regarding the significance of the Cosmic Christ in our time:

> Christ knows us. To a soul that sees our Spiritual Science in the true light, to a heart that feels it in its true significance, I can impart no more esoteric saying: *The Christ is seeing us.*
>
> (Dornach, November 1, 1915)

---

46. Rudolf Steiner, *From Jesus to Christ*, Rudolf Steiner Press, London, 1991. See especially lecture 10 for a discussion of the Christ as Lord of Karma.

1

Natural and Chance Illnesses in the Human Being

HAMBURG, MAY 20, 1910

THE CONTENT OF YESTERDAY'S LECTURE is very important, not only for what we will be considering next, but also for our understanding of karmic relationships in general.[1] Because of its crucial importance, let me briefly summarize the most important points.

We took as our starting point the fact that views on healing and medicines changed quite radically over the course of a relatively short time during the last century. We also pointed out that in the sixteenth and seventeenth centuries, a view developed based wholly on the premise that for each illness that had been named and conceptually delineated a cure could be found somewhere on Earth. People felt secure in the belief that if the appropriate medication were administered, it would necessarily affect the course of the illness. We then pointed out how this view persisted into the nineteenth century more or less; after that, however, it existed alongside its exact opposite. The opposing view was expressed in the nihilism of the Vienna school of medicine. This took as its point of departure the work of Dietl, the famous physician, and was taken further by Skoda and some of his students.[2] We described this nihilistic trend as beginning to have fundamental doubts about the absolute

1. Hamburg, May 19, 1910, "The Curability and Incurability of Diseases in Relation to Karma," *Manifestations of Karma*, Rudolf Steiner Press, London, 1969.
2. Joseph Skoda (1805–1881), a Czech Physician and diagnostician.

connection between an illness and any individual medication or treatment technique. Furthermore, knowledge of such a connection was no longer even wanted. The young physicians influenced by this school of thought arrived at the idea of so-called "self-healing." Very significantly for this school, Skoda himself stated that although we can diagnose and perhaps even explain and describe an illness, we have no means or medications with which to treat it.

This trend took as its starting point Dietl's demonstration that if an illness such as pneumonia were simply allowed to run its course, forces for self-healing would develop within a certain time period if the necessary circumstances were provided. He was able to demonstrate statistically that the same number of people were cured by (or died from) waiting out the illness as by administering the usual drugs. At that time the term "therapeutic nihilism" was not at all unjustified, since it was an absolute fact that the physicians of this school had no defense against their patients' conviction that there had to be an effective drug or prescription available. The patients were unrelenting, as was their environment—drugs had to be prescribed. Adherents of this school usually avoided the difficulty by prescribing a weak solution of gum arabic, since they believed it would have exactly the same effect as the drugs that had been formerly administered.

This taught us that the world of modern scientific fact is indeed impelling us to acknowledge what we may call one of life's karmic connections, since we had to answer to our own satisfaction the question of how so-called "self-healing" could occur. Or, to put it better, *why* does it come about? And why, in a different case, is self-healing (or any healing at all) impossible? If a whole school of thought, headed by a medical Greek chorus, so to speak, could resort to the idea of self-healing, any thinking person would have to conclude that something leading to overcoming illness is aroused in the course of the illness itself. This would then lead to tracking down the more obscure reasons behind the course of an illness.

We then tried to point out how this karmic connection with regard to the course an illness takes can be sought within the development of humanity. We showed that what we do in daily life—our good or bad deeds, our intelligent or senseless actions, our right or wrong attitudes—does not actually penetrate very far into the depths of the human organism. What underlies our moral, intellectual, and emotional judgments remains on the surface of our ordinary life and does not influence our organism's deeper forces. We then showed that there is a certain resistance to immorality penetrating our organism's deeper forces. This resistance, which keeps what we do and think from penetrating our system's forces, exists because we accompany our actions between birth and death with conscious ideas. This protects our organism by preventing the result of our actions from slipping down into it.

We then pointed out the significance of experiences that are irretrievably forgotten, and cannot possibly be pulled back up into our conscious life of ideas. We said that since in this case the protection afforded by ideas is missing, experiences such as these penetrate into our system in a certain way and influence its formative forces. We pointed out the types of illness that lie more on the surface—neuroses, neurasthenia, and so on; even hysteric conditions are illuminated by this viewpoint. We said that the causes of such conditions must be sought in ideas that have been forgotten and fallen out of awareness, but have sunk down inside us. As intruders from our soul life, they manifest in the form of illnesses.

We pointed to the incredible significance of the time between birth and the point at which we begin to remember our experiences, and noted how what we have forgotten continues to work within our living organism by bonding with our system's deeper forces, so to speak, influencing our organism from this vantage point. Thus, a complex of ideas or a series of experiences must sink deep down into the depths of our being before it can intervene in our organism.

We pointed out how this penetration is deepest when we have passed through the gate of death and are experiencing further existence between death and rebirth. Here, the qualitative aspect of all our experiences is transformed into forces that can then work in an organizing way. What we sensed and felt in the time between death and rebirth is assimilated into the sculpting forces that are involved in building up a new body as we enter a new existence. The formative forces that are now present are the result of what we formerly experienced in our soul life, and possibly even in our conscious ideas.

We were then able to point out that in our I-imbued life of ideas, we swing to and fro between two influences, the luciferic and the ahrimanic. When we commit a transgression that is called forth by qualities of the astral body, such as negative emotions or anger, we are being driven to act by luciferic powers. If these actions take the course described above and become formative forces for the body, we then find them underlying our new bodily existence as luciferic causes of illness.

We then saw how human beings are subject to the ahrimanic forces that work more from the outside inward. We had to acknowledge that ahrimanic influences are also transformed into formative forces, the forces that shape the newly built-up organism when a person enters existence at birth. To the extent that Ahriman's influences have mingled with the formative forces, we can speak of tendencies toward illnesses that are ahrimanic in character. We then went into detail. To clarify and sharply define our concept of this, I gave you radical examples of how these forces work. I asked you to imagine that a person has done everything in a preceding lifetime to cause a lack of self-confidence and a poor self-image; this person has prepared the I to relate nothing to itself, to lose itself in generalities, and so on. After death, such a person acquires the tendency to overcome that resistance and take up the forces that will enable him or her to strengthen and perfect the I later, during the course of incarnation. As a result, this person then seeks out circumstances that make it possible to do battle with certain forces, thus strengthening a poor self-image through having to put up resistance. It is true that such a tendency leads this person to seek out opportunities, as it were, to come down with cholera because this provides an opportunity to overcome resistance. Overcoming this resistance leads to a stronger self-image or to forces that allow a better self-image to develop gradually through self-discipline, either in the next incarnation or in the present one, in the event of recovery. We then said that in an illness such as malaria, we are presented with the opportunity to balance out an inflated self-image that has been cultivated by the soul through its actions and feelings in an earlier life.

Those of you who have participated in earlier discussions within the framework of our theosophical activity will be able to think this process through for yourselves. We have always said that a person's I finds its physical expression in the blood. Now, the two illnesses we have just mentioned both have to do with the blood and the laws governing it. In the case of cholera, a thickening of the blood takes place. This thickening is what we have described as the resistance that a weak self-image has to overcome, educating itself in the process. You can think through what happens in the case of malaria in the same way. In malaria, a disintegration of sorts takes place in the blood. An overly strong self-image needs the possibility of being taken to the point of absurdity, and when the blood is disintegrating, the exertions of an overly strong ego all come to naught. This is the opportunity presented by the disintegration of the blood. Of course the connections within our organism are extraordinarily subtle ones, but if you give them some time and attention, you will come to understand them.

From all of this we saw that when a person's organism is shaped by a soul that has the tendency to try to overcome something in a certain direction, this tendency leads the person to incorporate the opportunity to be ill and also to fight off the illness, since the possibility of a cure is the only reason to call forth the illness. And a cure takes place when a person's total karma is such that through overcoming the illness in question, the person acquires forces that really enable him or her to make progress through work on the physical plane for the remainder of life until death. That is, when the forces stimulated in this way are so strong that the person becomes able to accomplish on the physical plane what the illness was called forth to bring about, he or she goes on working with forces that were strengthened by the healing process and were not available before.

It may be that an individual's total karma is such that the intention is present to structure the organism in such a way as to receive forces that would lead toward wholeness now that the illness in question has been overcome. However, many different things are at work here, and the individual may have to let another aspect of the organism remain weak. In this case, the forces this person produces and applies in the healing process do bring strength, but not to the point of facilitating this individual's work on the physical plane. Since what has already been gained cannot be used on the physical plane, it will be applied when this person passes through the gate of death. The attempt will then be made to supplement his or her forces with what could not be added to them on the physical plane, so that they will be evident in the new body's formation at rebirth.

With this in mind, we must still point out what takes place in forms of illness that lead neither to a complete cure nor to death, but rather to a chronic condition, to a lasting infirmity, and so on. It is very important for most people to know this. In a case like this, the healing process in the human bodily sheaths has brought about something that can only be achieved if the illness has been overcome in a certain sense. In another sense, however, it has not been overcome. That is, everything that can be done to create a balance between the ether body and the physical body has been accomplished, but the lack of harmony between the ether body and the astral body has not been balanced out. This remains, and the person in question swings back and forth between attempting to find a cure and not being cured completely. In a case like this, it is always especially important for the individual to make full use of the healing that has actually been accomplished. However, this is very seldom what actually happens in life, because in an illness that becomes chronic, the patient is caught in a vicious cycle. In such a case, it would be a great help if the patient were in a position to isolate that part of the organism that has undergone a certain healing and let it live for itself, so to speak, separate from what is still rumbling around and out of order. (In such cases this usually lies more in the direction of the inner, soul aspect.) But many different things work against this possibility. For example, a person who has had some illness or other and has been left with a chronic condition, lives under the influence of that condition from then on. If I may put it crudely, this person can never fully forget about that condition, and never reaches a point where what is not yet healthy can be pulled away and treated separately. The person constantly thinks about the other part of the organism, and is compelled to bring the healthy part into some connection or other with the part that used to be sick, irritating it all over again.

This is a distinct process in itself, and in order to make this process clear to you, I would like to explain the spiritual-scientific state of affairs—what clairvoyant consciousness sees when someone has been through an illness and has retained a so-called chronic condition. By the way, the same thing happens when a chronic condition sets in without an acute illness ever having been apparent. In fact, it is then possible to see that in most such cases a certain shaky balance actually results between the ether body and the physical body; forces swing back and forth abnormally, but can be lived with. However, when the forces of the ether body and the physical body oscillate like this, this person will be constantly irritated and filled with agitation. Clairvoyant consciousness sees this appearing incessantly in the astral body, and these states of agitation continually force their way into the part of the system that is half sick, half healthy. Because of this, the balance that comes about is fragile rather than stable.

Because these astral states of agitation regularly force their way in, the person's condition, which could otherwise be much better, is actually very much aggravated. I ask you to take into account that *the astral* in this case does not coincide with consciousness, but primarily with agitated inner soul states which the patient does not want to acknowledge. In this case conditions and emotions such as mental shocks become overwhelmed by everything, and never being at peace, do not work like conscious forces, because the restraining effect of ideas is not present. Instead, these conditions operate like organizing forces or life forces that lie deeper within the human being and constantly irritate the aspect that is half-healthy, half-sick. If such people could actually manage, through strength of will or soul training, to forget about their condition, at least for a certain time, this would be a source of great satisfaction and would provide the strength they need to continue in this direction. They could forget about their condition, disregard it totally, and tell themselves with strong intent, "I am not going to worry about my condition now," and the soul forces freed up in this way could be applied to something with a spiritual content that would uplift them and satisfy their souls. If they were able to release the forces that are otherwise always engaged in feeling whatever dull or stabbing pain is present, this would be a great source of satisfaction, because when you are not experiencing these feelings, these forces are free for use at your discretion.

To be sure, it does not help much to simply say that you are not going to notice the aches and pains and so on, for if you do not apply the freed forces to something spiritual, your old condition will soon be back. However, if you take the forces that have been freed and apply them to a spiritual content that totally engages the soul, you will notice that you have accomplished in a complicated way what your organism otherwise does when it overcomes a disease process without your doing anything about it. Of course the people in question must be careful not to fill their souls in any way that is directly related to their illness. If someone who suffers from weak eyes, for instance, decides to stop thinking about this weakness by reading a lot in order to assimilate spiritual forces, this obviously cannot help accomplish that goal.

However, we don't need to use such far-fetched examples. Each of us can notice how much better it is when we are not feeling very well if we forget about how we are feeling by being occupied with something else. This is a positive, healthy kind of forgetting, and it is already an indication that we are not totally powerless when the karmic effects of transgressions in earlier lifetimes come to expression in illnesses. We recognize that what underlies the moral, emotional and intellectual consequences in our life between birth and death cannot go deep enough to become the cause of organic illness within our lifetime, but that during the time between death and rebirth it can penetrate deeply enough to cause illness; it must therefore also be possible to turn this process back into a conscious one!

We can also put the question like this: If illnesses come about as a karmic consequence of spiritual experiences or other experiences called forth by the soul—in other words, if illnesses are the transformation of these causes—isn't it conceivable, and don't spiritual facts tell us, that the result of this transformation, or illness, is avoidable to the extent that we substitute something else for this illness, which is called up out of our organic existence in order to educate us? Can't we replace the healing process with its spiritual equivalent? If we are clever enough, can't we transform the illness into a spiritual process and use our soul forces to carry out the self-education we were meant to undergo through the illness?

I would like to give you another example to illustrate that something like this really belongs to the realm of fact. I must say again at this point that I will only present examples that have been investigated by spiritual-scientific means. These are real cases and not merely a hypothesis that is being put forth. And because these are not hypothetical examples, you cannot expect completeness from me; they are actual cases that must be taken as they are.

Let's assume that a certain person comes down with measles rather later in life, and that we are looking for the karmic connection in this case. We find that this case of measles has appeared as a karmic consequence of processes in a preceding life that can be described somewhat as follows: In a preceding life, the individual in question did not like to be bothered with the outer world and was very occupied with herself, although not in a crudely egotistical sense. This was a personality who did a lot of investigating and thinking, but not about the facts of the outer world. She restricted herself to the inner life of the soul. Today, too, we find very many people who believe that they can arrive at the solution to the riddles of the world by shutting themselves up within themselves and brooding. The person I am talking about tried to come to grips with life through inwardness, by brooding on how one ought to behave in specific instances. That lifetime resulted in a weakened soul, and in the life between death and rebirth forces were created that subjected this person's organism to measles relatively late in life.

On the one hand, we have an attack of measles, which is the physical karmic consequence of an earlier life. On the other hand, we can now ask about the state of this person's soul, because an earlier lifetime also causes a particular soul condition as a karmic consequence. This soul condition is such that, during the life in which she contracted the measles, the personality in question was subject to self-deception over and over again. Her self-deceptions must be seen as that earlier life's karmic consequence for her soul, and the appearance of the measles as its physical karmic consequence.

Now let's suppose that this personality had been fundamentally successful in doing something to better her condition before the attack of measles occurred. If, through self-education, she had acquired such inner strength that she was no longer subject to all kinds of self-deceptions, the illness would have been unnecessary, because what was called forth in her physical organism when it was being formed would have found a balance in the stronger soul forces developed through self-discipline.

Of course I cannot go on talking about these things for six months, but if you look around at all the details of the experiences that life presents and consider them from the starting point provided here, you will find that outer knowledge confirms what has been said here in all its details. And what I have just said about this case of measles can lead to points of view that explain why measles in particular is one of the common childhood illnesses. The qualities I have indicated occur in many lives, and there are certain periods when they have been rampant. When such a personality enters existence, he or she will want to bring about a correction in this area as quickly as possible. During the time between birth and the usual appearance of childhood illnesses, a person will come down with measles in order to exercise self-discipline by organic means, since there is usually no question of the soul educating itself at this age.

You can see from this that it really is possible to speak of changing an illness back into a spiritual process in a certain respect. It is extremely significant that if the soul takes up this process as a motto for life, this engenders a way of looking at things that has a healing effect on the soul. In our time, we need not be particularly surprised that there is so little possibility to affect souls. If we look at our present time from a spiritual-scientific viewpoint, we will understand why so many physicians become materialists, why they despair of any soul influence: The majority of people are not at all involved in anything with any fructifying power. None of that stuff in popular literature possesses any forces fruitful for the soul.

This is why anyone wanting to work on behalf of spiritual science will find our theosophical activity to be something that is health-bringing in the highest sense, because spiritual-scientific knowledge can once again bring something to humanity that pours into the soul in such a way as to turn it away from the forces that shape the physical body. However, we must not confuse what appears during the initial phase of a movement such as ours with what that movement can really become. In fact, things that are rampant in the outer world are brought into the theosophical movement.[3] When people become theosophists, they approach theosophy with many of the same interests they have outside the movement, as well as with all the bad habits they possess outside. Much of the shadow side of our age is brought in. But when shadowy aspects then become apparent in such people, others say that theosophy caused this, which is, of course, a very cheap and easy way to look at it.

When we see the karmic threads being drawn from one incarnation into the next, we have only grasped one side of the truth. For someone who has acquired a feeling for how karmic threads run

3. At the time of this lecture, Rudolf Steiner was the head of the Adyar Branch of the German Section of the Theosophical Society. Earlier Steiner had begun moving in a new direction of spiritual-scientific research, and in 1913 his students founded the Anthroposophical Society. He continued to use the term "theosophy" in its original meaning—i.e., from the Greek words, *theos*, meaning god or deity, and *sophy*, meaning wisdom.

from incarnation to incarnation, many questions arise. We will touch on these questions in the course of these lectures. Above all, we must consider the question of how to distinguish between an illness with outer causes and one that is inherent in a person's system. We may feel that we resolve the matter by stating that the illness appeared on its own without any outer cause. Of course this is not absolutely the case, but from a certain point of view we are justified in saying that there are illnesses that appear simply because the person in question is especially predisposed to them inwardly.

On the other hand, it is possible for us to demonstrate outer causes for many illnesses. This is not true of everything, but for many things that happen to us from outside—breaking a leg, for instance—we must take external causes into account. We must also take outer causes into account in what happens as a result of weather conditions, as well as in the many cases of illness due to poor living conditions in cities. This opens up a whole new area to consider. For an experienced person looking around in the world, it now becomes understandable why the fashionable trend in medicine seeks the causes of disease in outside influences, especially germs. Some clever person once said, and not unjustifiably, that illnesses nowadays come from germs, while we used to say that they come from God or from the devil. In the thirteenth century, people said that illnesses came from God; in the fifteenth century, that they came from the devil. Later, it was said that they came from "humors," and today we say that they come from germs. These are the different points of view that have succeeded each other over the course of time.

It is clear that we need to speak of outer causes of human health or illness, and in this connection modern people are easily tempted to use a word that is basically very well suited to disrupting our entire view of the world. If someone who was formerly quite healthy enters an area infected with influenza or diphtheria and becomes ill, a person today will certainly be inclined to say that this individual was exposed to the germs of that illness by coming into the infected area. The word "chance" will then easily come to mind. Nowadays it is easy to talk about chance, or coincidental effects. Many world-views have been crucified on the "cross" of chance. And as long as we do not even attempt to gain a bit of clarity on what we so easily call *chance*, we will not be able to move on to any relatively satisfying view of the world. We are now at the beginning of the chapter on "Natural and Chance Illnesses in the Human Being." There is no way around it; today we must make an initial attempt to shed some light on the term "chance."

Isn't it true that chance itself is something that could make us suspicious of what we so easily think when we hear the word? In an earlier lecture, I pointed out that a wise man in the eighteenth century was not altogether wrong in stating that rather than erecting monuments to great explorers and inventors and so on, as is the custom, most of our monuments would be dedicated to Chance if we considered the course of history objectively. Strangely enough, when we go into history in detail, we can make surprising discoveries about what lies concealed behind "chance." I once told you that we owe the invention of the telescope to a game children were playing in an optician's workshop; because of a combination that came about as they were playing with the lenses, someone managed to invent the telescope. We could also point to the famous chandelier in the cathedral at Pisa. Although it had been swinging with the same regularity for years in full view of thousands and thousands of people, Galileo was the first to find that its oscillations coincided with his pulse, and thus discovered the laws governing the pendulum. Without these laws, our entire culture would have taken a different direction. Try to look for a meaning in the course of humanity's development, and then see if you still want to say Galileo was led to this important discovery through mere chance.

Let us now consider a different case, and the significance of Luther's translation of the Bible for the civilized countries of Europe. Let's make it clear to ourselves what a profound influence it had, not only on religious feeling and thought, but also on the development of a German literary language. I only want to emphasize that it had this profound influence, and present it as a fact without talking about it. You must now try to see the meaning of the education of humanity that has occurred over several centuries as a result of Luther's translation of the Bible. Then, having tried to see a meaning in this, take all the intelligent things you have to say about the significance of developments that have taken place since the sixteenth and seventeenth centuries, and place them beside the following fact: Up to a certain point in his life, Luther had been deeply involved in everything that could guide his own personality toward becoming a "child of God" through reading the Bible. He had switched from the Augustinian preference for reading the church fathers to the enjoyment of reading the Bible itself. Everything was now ready for this state of being a "child of God" to flame up as an all-encompassing emotion in his soul. This was his perspective in applying himself to his teaching post in theology during his first period at Wittenberg. I now want to emphasize that Luther had a certain resistance to acquiring the title of Doctor of Theology, but during a coincidental conversation while sitting with an old friend from the Erfurt Augustinian monastery, he was really persuaded to do it after all. However, for him that meant taking up the study of the Bible again. So sitting together with his friend led quite by chance to a renewed study of the Bible and to everything that then came to expression because of it.

Consider what this means concerning the last few centuries, and try to link it to the fact that Luther once sat with a friend and let himself be talked into becoming a doctor of theology. You will be forced to make a strangely grotesque association between the historical development's significance and the chance event.

You may gather from what has been said thus far that the significance of chance may be somewhat different from what we usually think it is. We usually think of chance as something that cannot be totally explained by natural laws, by the laws of life, so to speak—as something that is in excess of what can be explained, as it were. Now take, in addition to what has just been said, a fact that has already helped us understand so many aspects of life—namely, that for the duration of our earthly existence, we human individualities are subject to the two forces of the luciferic and ahrimanic principles. These forces and principles are constantly playing into us. The luciferic forces work more by taking hold of us inside, in our astral body, while the ahrimanic forces work more through what we receive by way of outer impressions. The ahrimanic forces are present in what we receive from the outer world, and the luciferic forces are present in what rises up in our souls and takes effect as pleasure or displeasure, emotions, and so on.

Now, both the luciferic and the ahrimanic principles lead us to give ourselves up to illusions. The luciferic principle causes us to be subject to illusions about our own inner aspect, to being capable of misjudging our own inner being and beholding an illusion within ourselves. It will not be difficult for you to become aware of this *maya* in your own soul life if you consider it rationally. Try to observe how infinitely often people persuade themselves that they are doing something or other for one or the other reason. Usually they are doing it for a totally different and more deep-seated reason, but in their superficial consciousness they explain an action to which they are driven by anger or passion in a totally different way. Having done something that the world does not regard highly, they try to banish it by decree, ordering it gone. And when people are driven to do something by thoroughly egotistical emotions, you can often experience that they cloak crudely egotistical urges in an unegotistical mantle by explaining why it had to happen. Usually they do not know that this is what they are doing. When they do know, they usually feel a certain shame that indicates the beginning of improvement. Worst of all, people are driven to do something out of the depths of their soul and then think up a motive for having done it. Modern psychologists have also noticed this. But simply because so little psychological education currently takes place, these truths undergo a grotesque development at the hands of today's materialistic psychologists. They arrive at some very peculiar interpretations of life.

Spiritual investigators who notice such a fact will, of course, see through it to its true significance and characterize it as the interaction of two things: our consciousness, and what prevails in the depths beneath the threshold of consciousness. However, materialistic psychologists who notice it will deal with the matter quite differently. They will immediately start cooking up a theory about the difference between a person's excuse for an action and the actual motive. When psychologists talk about the suicides so prevalent among schoolchildren today, they say that the pretexts given for them are not the real motives, that the real motives lie much deeper, usually in misdirected sexual activity which is then transformed in such a way as to present the consciousness with some feigned reasons or other.

Such reasoning can often be correct, but no one touched by truly profound psychological thinking would ever make a comprehensive theory of it. Such a theory can easily be disproved, because we would have to think that if it is really true that the excuse is nothing and the motive everything, this would also have to apply to these psychologists. We would have to say to them, "All right, if we are looking for deeper reasons, what you are presenting and developing as a theory right now is only a pretext; perhaps your so-called reasons are only pretexts, too." If these psychologists had really learned why it is impossible to judge on the basis of a conclusion such as "All Cretans are liars," and that this judgment proves false as soon as a Cretan says it—if they had learned why this is so, they would also have learned what kind of strange, circular arguments result when you apply your own assertions to yourself in certain areas. This is why it will be especially important for spiritual science to avoid such similarly logical confusion in every respect. Modern philosophers who are concerned with psychology are the least likely to avoid such confusion. Our example is typical of that, and it allows us to see the tricks played on us by luciferic influences, which transform our soul life into a *maya* so that we are capable of pretending that our motives are quite different from the ones that really prevail within us.

This is an area in which we should try to implement stricter self-discipline. It is usually very easy these days to handle words, but words are also terribly seductive. When words merely sound nice and give even the slightest impression that a sentence represents a beneficial action, then the nice-sounding sentence is already seducing us into believing that the motive in question is present in our soul, when in fact, the egotistic principle can stand behind it. We do not necessarily even have an inkling of this, because we do not have the will to engage in real self-knowledge.

This is how we see Lucifer working; but how is Ahriman working? Ahriman is the principle that mingles with our perceptions and insinuates itself from outside. Now, Ahriman works most strongly in cases where we have the feeling that we can no longer follow through with our thinking, that we are at a critical point in our thinking where our thoughts get all tangled up. At this point the ahrimanic principle seizes the opportunity to get inside us, as if through a crack in the outer world. If we follow the course of world events and look at the more apparent ones, such as tracing modern physics back to the moment when Galileo sat in front of the swinging chandelier in the Pisa cathedral, we can spin a web of thoughts over all events and explain things to ourselves easily. Wherever we turn, things will be explainable. But at the point where we arrive at the swinging chandelier, our thoughts get confused. This is the window through which the ahrimanic forces can enter most strongly, and it is here that our thinking ceases to understand the aspect of the phenomena that can bring reason and understanding to bear on the matter. However, this is also where we come up against what we call "chance." It is to be found right there where Ahriman becomes most dangerous. It is through the phenomena we call "coincidence" or "chance" that we are most easily fooled by the ahrimanic influence.

Thus we will learn to understand that in those cases where we feel obliged to speak of "chance," this does not lie in the nature of the facts themselves but rather in us, in our own development. We will gradually have to educate ourselves to penetrate maya or illusion—that is, to penetrate things at the point where Ahriman works most strongly. Where we have to speak about important causes of illness and about shedding light on the source of many illnesses, we will need to tackle the phenomena from this angle. We will first attempt to understand to what extent it is not by chance that a person takes the particular train on which he or she suffers a fatal accident, or what the situation is when a person is exposed to a germ working from outside or to some other cause of illness at a particular time. If we sharpen our understanding of the things we are pursuing, we will then be in a position to have a more profound understanding of the true nature and the whole significance of illness and wellness in our life.

In today's lecture, I needed to show at some length how Lucifer leads to illusion within the human being, while Ahriman mingles with our outer perceptions and leads to maya there; how it is an effect of Lucifer when people convince themselves that they are acting out of a motive that is in fact false; and how false assumptions with regard to the world of phenomena—deception by Ahriman—lead us to the conclusion that something happens by "chance." I had to create this foundation before showing how karmic events, the results of earlier lives, are also at work in the human being, explaining phenomena in which outer circumstances work to bring about illness, seemingly by chance.[4]

---

4. For a lecture specifically related to karma and illness see: Rudolf Steiner. *Karmic Relationships: Esoteric Studies*, vol. 1, Rudolf Steiner Press, London, 1972, lecture 5, March 1, 1924. For further reading on the anthroposophical view of illness and medicine, the following books will be of interest:

Dr. Michael Evans and Iain Rodger. *Anthroposophical Medicine: Healing for Body, Soul and Spirit*. Thorsons, London, 1992.

L.C.F. Mees, MD. *Blessed By Illness*. Anthroposophic Press, Hudson, NY, 1983.

Rudolf Steiner. *Fundamentals of Anthroposophic Medicine*. Mercury Press, Spring Valley, NY, 1986.

—— *Geographic Medicine and The Double: Two Lectures*. Mercury Press, Spring Valley, NY, 1979.

—— *Health and Illness, Volume 2: Lectures to the Workmen*. Anthroposophic Press, Hudson, NY, 1983.

—— *Nutrition and Health: Two Lectures to Workmen*. Anthroposophic Press, Hudson, NY, 1987.

2

Elemental Events, Volcanic Eruptions, Earthquakes, and Epidemics in Relation to Karma

HAMBURG, MAY 22, 1910

You have already seen in these lectures that we are approaching our goal one step at a time and attempting to penetrate the subject more deeply with each step we take. My last lecture was about the nature of the pain associated with the course of an illness.[1] However, we also realized that there are cases where an illness can run its course—at least in some respects—without being accompanied by the experience of pain.

We must now go into the nature of pain somewhat more exactly. Once again, we must keep in mind that it is possible for pain to appear as a phenomenon that runs parallel to illness, since we have seen from our earlier considerations that we cannot regard illness and pain as belonging together. We must keep in mind that when pain is associated with an illness, something other than simply the diseased condition must come into play.

We have already become aware that in the transition from one incarnation to another, when experiences from earlier incarnations are being transformed into causes of illness, both the luciferic principle on the one hand and the ahrimanic principle on the other are involved. How do we actually lay the foundation for disease

---

1. Lecture of May 21, "Relationships between Karma and Accidents," *Manifestations of Karma*, Rudolf Steiner Press, London, 1969.

processes? Why do we assimilate the tendency to become ill? We have described the time between death and rebirth as the time in which the forces that cause illness are consolidated. During this time, what leads us to prepare the forces that are then played out in illness in our next life? It is the tendency to succumb to the temptations of the luciferic power on the one hand and of the ahrimanic power on the other.

We already know what it means to succumb to the luciferic power: Everything that works in us as desire, everything that is characteristic of self-seeking, ambition, arrogance, vanity—all those qualities that have to do with our I putting on airs and asserting itself in an especially strong way—all this has to do with the temptation of the luciferic powers within us. In other words, if we succumb to the forces that work in our astral body, and if they express themselves in our having egotistical desires and passions, then during the incarnation in question we perform actions that have been dictated by the temptation of Lucifer. Later during the time between death and rebirth, we experience the result of these actions influenced by Lucifer and assimilate the tendency to reincarnate in such a way that we go through a disease process. If we overcome this, it can contribute to our freeing ourselves from the clutches of these luciferic powers. Thus, if the luciferic powers were not present, we could not succumb to the temptations that lead us to assimilate these forces.

If the only thing existing in life were what Lucifer brings about in us, causing us to develop certain egotistical urges and passions, then we would actually never be able to escape from the luciferic temptations during one lifetime. We would also not be able to escape from them during successive incarnations because we would succumb to them every time. For example, if we were simply left to our own devices and to the luciferic influence throughout Earth's evolution, we would have the temptations of the luciferic powers during one incarnation, and after death perceive where they had led us. We would then bring about a disease process. However, if there were really nothing else that came into play, this disease process would not lead to any particular improvement during the lifetime in which it occurred. It only leads to improvement because the powers opposed by Lucifer add something else to this whole process. Thus, when we succumb to the luciferic powers on the one hand, the opponents of the luciferic powers intervene with the opposite effect, attempting to develop a counterforce that can really drive the luciferic influence out of us. And what these opposing powers add to the process that comes about under the influence of Lucifer, is *pain*. We must therefore look at pain as something contributed by the good powers—if we call the luciferic powers evil—so that through pain, we can wrest ourselves from the clutches of the evil powers and no longer succumb to them. If the disease process that results from our succumbing to the luciferic powers did not involve pain, we would have the experience that succumbing to these powers is really not so bad! There would be nothing in us that would lead us to apply our forces to tearing ourselves away from the luciferic powers. Pain means becoming conscious of an astral body that is growing improperly, and it is also what can prevent us from continuing to surrender to the luciferic powers in an area where we have already succumbed to them. In this way, pain educates us with regard to the temptations of the luciferic powers.

There is no point in asking how pain can educate us if we only experience it within ourselves without becoming aware of its beneficial force. Not becoming aware of its positive force is only a consequence of our I-consciousness. Even though we know nothing about it in our everyday consciousness, in the consciousness I have described as lying below the level of I-consciousness, we experience pain as the concurrence of what the good powers contribute to counteract our shortcomings. This is a force in our subconscious that works as karmic fulfillment, as an impulse to succumb no longer to the actions, urges and desires that have called forth this particular illness.

Thus we see how karma works: We submit to the luciferic powers, and they give us an illness in our next incarnation. We also see how the benevolent powers add pain to what would otherwise simply be damage to our organs, and how this pain serves as a subconscious means of education. Therefore, we can say that wherever pain appears with an illness, the power that has caused this illness is a luciferic power. In fact, pain is an indicator of a luciferic power underlying the illness.

People who enjoy being analytical will now feel the need to distinguish between illnesses based solely on luciferic influence and those that can be attributed solely to ahrimanic influence. In all theoretical activities, analysis and schematization are the easiest things to do, and we think they explain a lot. But in reality, things don't behave in such a way that we can use these easy and convenient means of understanding them. Instead, they are constantly intersecting and merging. It will be easy enough for us to grasp that in an actual disease process, part of it can be attributed to luciferic influence—that is, we can look for these things more in the qualities of our astral body—and another part to things that can be found in ahrimanic influence. We may not assume that if something hurts, this is due to Lucifer's influence alone. That we are in pain only shows us the part of the illness that can be attributed to luciferic influence. But we will understand this more easily if we ask ourselves where the ahrimanic influence comes from.

Human beings would not have succumbed to ahrimanic influence at all if they had not first succumbed to luciferic influence. Taking the luciferic influence into ourselves brought about a connection between our four members: physical body, ether body, astral body, and I. Such a connection would not have existed if Lucifer had not been active, if the only powers at work had been the ones Lucifer opposes. In that case, we would have evolved differently. The luciferic principle therefore caused an inner disturbance in us. What is inside of us, however, determines how we allow the outer world to approach us. If something has been destroyed in your eye, you cannot see the outer world correctly because of the inner flaw. Similarly, because of the luciferic influence, we do not see the outer world at all as it really is.

With this as a basis, the ahrimanic influence was then able to invade our incorrect image of the outer world. Therefore, Ahriman could only approach the human being because the luciferic influence had taken effect first. Because of the ahrimanic influence, not only is it possible for us to submit to egotistical passions, urges and desires such as vanity and arrogance, but, within a human organism where egotism is working like this, it is also possible for organs to develop that can only see the outer world in a distorted and incorrect way. That is how Ahriman has been able to mingle with our incorrect images of the outer world. Ahriman approached, subjecting us to a different influence; as a result, we can succumb not only to inner temptations but also to errors in assessing the outer world and to lying about it. While it is true that Ahriman works from outside, it is also true that we initially gave him the possibility to approach us.

And so the ahrimanic and luciferic influences never stand alone. They are always affecting each other, keeping each other in balance in a certain way. Lucifer forces his way outward from within, Ahriman works in from outside, and our image of the world takes shape between the two. If in any given incarnation the inner human being becomes stronger—if we become more subject to inner influences—then we submit more to the luciferic influence in those things within us that cause us to be consumed with arrogance, vanity and so on. In an incarnation where our overall karma makes us less subject to inner influences, we can more easily succumb to the errors and temptations of Ahriman. This is how things truly are in our life. As we make our way through life on a day-to-day basis, we fall prey more easily to Lucifer's temptations at one moment, to Ahriman's at another. We swing back and forth between these two, as they lead us on the one hand to inner self-inflation, and on the other to deceiving ourselves with illusions about the outer world.

At this point it is extremely important to mention that people who are striving for higher development and to enter the spiritual worlds either by breaking through the appearances of the outer world and into the spiritual, or through a mystical descent into themselves—must make a special effort to resist the temptations coming from both sides. When we penetrate the spiritual outer world that lies behind the physical world, Ahriman is always trying to pull the wool over our eyes with deceptive images. When we want to descend into our own souls, the possibility of being tempted by Lucifer is greater than usual.

When people become mystics and strive blissfully inward without taking precautions to counteract arrogance, vanity, and so on by developing their personal character, when they succeed in living like mystics without particularly cultivating morality, they are more likely to succumb to Lucifer's temptations, which work into their souls from within. Thus, mystics who have paid little attention to cultivating morality, and who succeed in penetrating their inner being to a slight extent, are in great danger of experiencing a setback at the hand of luciferic influence, becoming even more vain and arrogant than they were before. This is why it is necessary to develop one's character beforehand, to counteract the temptations to vanity, arrogance, and delusions of grandeur that will invariably present themselves. We cannot do enough to acquire the personal qualities that lead to modesty and humility. Above all, this is important for what we call the mystical side of our higher development.

When we are trying to reach the primal spiritual foundations of things through a personal development that leads beyond the appearances of the outer world, we must also protect ourselves from Ahriman's delusionary creations on the other side. In this case, if we do not try to achieve a development of character that makes us inwardly strong and powerful, that allows us to build securely on our inner being, it can very easily happen that we succumb to Ahriman, who pulls the wool over our eyes with illusions and hallucinations. This is especially likely when we actually succeed in getting into the spiritual world.

It often happens that people like me are taken "at their word" in a certain respect. Because we have so often emphasized that any higher development aimed at getting beyond the world's outer appearances must be accomplished with full consciousness, people bring us semi-somnambulant individuals who declare that they do indeed perceive the spiritual world in full consciousness. In these cases, all we can say is, "It would be much wiser if you didn't want to be conscious!" These people are mistaken about their "consciousness." Theirs is a mere image-consciousness or astral-consciousness, since if they were not less than fully conscious, they would not perceive these things. But the point is to maintain I-consciousness when entering the spiritual world, and I-consciousness is bound up with the strength to assess things and the ability to distinguish clearly. These people do not have this ability with regard to the figures they see in the spiritual world. Having some kind of consciousness is not admirable in itself. The consciousness bound up with the cultivation of our I is the one we need to have.

This is why, with regard to developing a perception of higher worlds, the emphasis is not on getting into a higher world as quickly as possible and seeing all kinds of figures or perhaps hearing all kinds of voices. Rather, it is emphasized that entering the spiritual world can only be a positive and advantageous experience if we first sharpen our consciousness, our ability to make distinctions, and our powers of judgment. There is no better way to do this than by studying spiritual science. This is why we emphasize that working with spiritual-scientific truths offers protection against supposedly seeing all kinds of figures we cannot comprehend with our powers of judgment. Those who are really trained in this way will not mistake one arbitrary phenomenon for another, but will be able to distinguish between reality and foggy images. Above all, it will be clear to them that it is especially necessary to be careful with things appearing as perceptions of hearing, because a perception of hearing can never be correct if the person in question has not first passed through the sphere of absolute stillness.

Those who have not experienced the absolute stillness and silence of the spiritual world can say with confidence that they are perceiving deceptive images, regardless of what clever things these images may tell them. Only those who have made an effort to strengthen their power of judgment by trying to understand the truths of higher worlds can defend themselves against illusory images. The methods of external science are inadequate for this. External science does not supply the keen and strengthening power of judgment that is necessary in order to truly make distinctions in a spiritual world. Therefore, when people who have not carefully sharpened their powers of judgment try to communicate something from higher worlds, these communications are always extremely debatable and must first, at the very least, be checked according to methods requiring a genuine schooling.

Lucifer draws back from only one force, and that is morality. Morality burns Lucifer like the most terrible fire. And there is no means of working against Ahriman other than through powers of judgment schooled in spiritual science, and ability to make distinctions. Ahriman flees in terror from what we have acquired on Earth through healthy powers of judgment. His greatest aversion is to what we acquire through a healthy training of our I-consciousness. We will see that Ahriman belongs to a realm that is totally different and far removed from what we develop by cultivating a healthy capacity for judgment. When Ahriman meets with healthy judgment achieved in earthly existence, he gets a terrible shock, because to him this is something unknown and very frightening. Therefore, the more effort we make to develop a healthy capacity for judgment in the life between birth and death, the more we work to counteract Ahriman. This is especially apparent in the various persons brought to meet someone like me, who then "talk a blue streak" about all the spiritual worlds they have seen. If you make even the slightest attempt to clarify something for these individuals, to teach them understanding and discrimination, they can scarcely pursue it because Ahriman usually has them so strongly in his power. And the more Ahriman's temptations are expressed acoustically, the stronger this becomes.

There are more means of counteracting visionary images than there are against acoustic manifestations, such as voices that are heard and so on. Such people are averse to learning what needs to be acquired for I-consciousness between birth and death. They dislike it. But it is not they themselves who dislike it; ahrimanic powers pull them away from it. However, if such people reach the point of developing healthy powers of judgment and begin to accept instruction, it often happens that the voices and hallucinations cease, since they were only foggy ahrimanic images to begin with. Ahriman gets terribly afraid when he feels a healthy power of judgment proceeding from a person.

In fact, the best treatment for the especially damaging illness that consists of visions and hallucinatory hearing induced by Ahriman, is for these people to acquire a healthy and rational capacity for judgment. They are trapped because one power makes things very comfortable for them while the other power leads them on. However, anyone who wants to drive this power out cannot be so comfortable. It is really difficult to get through to individuals like this, because they insist that you have deprived them of what used to lead them up into the spiritual world, while in truth you have made them healthy and prevented these powers from acquiring more and more power over them.

So now we have seen the great dislikes of the luciferic and ahrimanic powers. Lucifer's greatest aversion is to modesty in people, to their refusal to think more highly of themselves than sound judgment would justify. On the other hand, Lucifer is there like flies in a dirty room wherever traits such as ambition or vanity are trying to emerge. These things, especially the things that rest on our mistaken ideas about ourselves, also prepare us for Ahriman. However, nothing protects us against Ahriman better than making a real effort during our lifetime to think soundly, in the way that life between death and birth teaches us. And especially those with a foundation in spiritual science have reason to emphasize again and again, with all possible intensity, that it is not to our credit as earthly individuals to disregard what earthly life is supposed to give us. Those who scorn the acquisition of sound judgment and rational discrimination, who want to do without them and ascend to a spiritual world the easy way, simply want to withdraw from earthly life. They want to float above earthly life. They find it demeaning to have to deal with all kinds of things that can lead to an understanding of earthly life. They think they are better than that. Such a feeling, however, is a new reason for arrogance. That is why we can see again and again that certain individuals with visionary tendencies—people who do not want to be touched by earthly things and earthly life, and refuse to learn because they are "already there, after all—do not want to support our movement, yet these are the people who say that humankind must enter the spiritual world!

That is true, of course, but there is only one healthy way to enter it: namely the morality we have worked to achieve on Earth—morality in a higher sense, morality that does not allow us to overestimate ourselves or come to false conclusions about ourselves, and that also does not allow us to be dependent on our urges, desires, and passions. Such morality is an industrious, healthy collaboration with life's earthly circumstances, not a desire to float above them.

With this, we have brought something up from the depths of karma that is deeply connected with spiritual life. It can be of great value. But nothing is of value for the development of a person's individuality if it is brought from the spiritual world without healthy, rational understanding. If brought without morality, it is also of no value. We can see this from the facts presented both yesterday and today, and we can ask: Why not? Just because the luciferic influence was at work initially, and was then transformed into illness and balanced out by pain, why shouldn't it pull the ahrimanic influence along behind it, as it were? And why shouldn't the ahrimanic influence—a consequence of the luciferic influence—be involved in the cause of pain and show us the luciferic course of an illness? But how does the ahrimanic influence work, and how are Ahriman's temptations transformed into the causes of illness? How does this appear in a later incarnation?

It is true that what is due to the ahrimanic influence can be traced back to Lucifer indirectly. However, although the luciferic influence was so strong that it called forth the ahrimanic influence, the ahrimanic influence is more insidious. It is more deeply seated and lies not only in the shortcomings of the astral body, but in those of the ether body, as well. The ahrimanic influence appears at a level of consciousness lying below the level of our awareness of pain. It causes damage that is not necessarily accompanied by pain, but makes the damaged organ unusable.

Let us assume that an ahrimanic influence has been at work in one incarnation, and has called forth what only it can call forth. Now the person in question lives through the time between death and rebirth and reappears in a new incarnation. It then becomes evident that some organ or other has been taken hold of by ahrimanic activity or, in other words, that the ether body is located much deeper inside this organ than it should be. In such a case, having this defective organ will lead the person to get even more tangled up in error, which is what Ahriman brings about in the world. Because of this organ with its deep-seated ether body and the damage done to it by the ahrimanic influence, if this person wanted to go through the whole process, the result would be ever more entanglement in the *maya* that Ahriman can cause. However, because what the outer world generates as *maya* cannot be taken along into the spiritual world, the spiritual world withdraws from this individual more and more, since in the spiritual world there is only truth and no illusion. The more entangled the person becomes in the illusion brought about by Ahriman, the more this individual is forced to shift to the sense-perceptible outer world, to physical, sense-perceptible illusion, to a much greater extent than would have been the case if without a defective organ.

Here, too, however, a counter-effect appears, just as a counter-effect appears in the form of pain in the case of the luciferic influence. Here, the counter-effect appears as the destruction of a particular organ at the moment we are in danger of chaining ourselves too strongly to the physical, sense-perceptible world, and of depriving ourselves of too much of what could lead us up into the spiritual world. At this moment the organ is destroyed. It is either paralyzed, or made too weak to function. A destructive process sets in. We must realize that when we see that an organ has been destroyed, we actually have the benevolent powers to thank for taking this organ away from us so that we can find our way back to the spiritual world. If this cannot happen by any other means, then in fact organs are destroyed by certain powers, or we are supplied with diseased organs, so that we are not driven too deeply into illusion.

If we have a liver disease that as such is not accompanied by any experience of pain, this has to do with the effect of a prior ahrimanic influence that has caused damage to the liver. If this organ were not taken away from us, we would be led to a greater entanglement with *maya* by the forces that are bound up with the deeper penetration of the ether body.

Legends and myths have always known and expressed the deepest wisdom. The liver in particular is a good example of this, because it is one of the organs that can most easily work to smooth the way for us to enter the physical illusory world. And at the same time, the liver is the organ that actually binds us to Earth. This truth is related to the legend of Prometheus, the being who brought human beings a power that was intended to lead them into earthly life and make them highly effective in it. Prometheus had a vulture gnawing at his liver, not in order to cause him great pain, because in that case the legend would not agree with the actual facts. But legends always agree with the physiological facts. The vulture was gnawing at his liver because that did *not* cause pain! This was intended to point out that Prometheus brought something to humankind that could entangle us more deeply with Ahriman unless an opposing, balancing effect could come about. Esoteric documents are always in harmony with the truths we promulgate in spiritual science.

Today, purely on the basis of the issue itself, I have shown you that the good powers subject us to pain in order to counteract the influence of Lucifer. Now bring this into relationship with the Old Testament. When Lucifer's influence had taken place, as symbolized for us in the snake that tempted Eve, the opponents of Lucifer imposed pain on what Lucifer was trying to bring to human beings. The power Lucifer opposes had to come and speak about pain being brought to humanity. Yahweh or Jehovah does this, saying, "In pain you shall bear your children."

As a rule, we don't know how to interpret these things in the esoteric documents as long as we do not yet have spiritual-scientific explanations as such. It is only afterward that we realize how profound these documents are. This is also why you cannot ask me to explain things without any further ado, out of nothing, without the appropriate preparation. To be able to speak at all about the words "In pain you shall bear your children," we must first consider karma, because the explanation of this passage can only be inserted at the appropriate point. This is why it is not very useful to want to have one thing or another from occult documents explained before reaching the right moment in one's esoteric development. It is always unfortunate when people ask, "What does that mean?" We must always wait and have patience until the right moment has come; there is nothing to be accomplished by explanations alone.

Thus we see the luciferic powers working into our life, and at the same time, the powers opposed by Lucifer. Then the ahrimanic forces work into our life, and we must understand that the powers that make organs unusable for us when we succumb to Ahriman's influence are to be counted among the good powers opposed by Ahriman.

If you take what has now been said as your starting point, you will see deep into the complicated workings of human nature, and you will realize that the luciferic powers are those that lagged behind during the Old Moon period. Within the evolution of our Earth, they now work into human life using forces that are actually Moon forces. In a cosmic plan that included only those powers opposed by Lucifer, these forces would have no place at all in our earthly evolution. Lucifer is intervening in another being's plan.

However, we can also go back to still more distant evolutionary epochs. When we see that some beings on the Moon remained behind in their development in order to intervene in human life on Earth, it will also seem understandable to us that other beings lagged behind on Old Sun, beings who then played a role on the

Moon similar to that now played by the luciferic beings on Earth. Today we find something we can actually describe as a battle going on within the human being, a battle taking place between the luciferic powers who settle into our astral body and the powers that work on us through our I, through what we have acquired on Earth. These powers opposed by Lucifer can only work on us by means of our I. We acquire clarity and a correct estimation of ourselves only with the help of these powers that work on our I, and we must use our I for this to happen. We can therefore say that when our I resists luciferic powers, Yahweh or Jehovah is fighting Lucifer in us. What looks after the cosmic plan for the good is fighting against what resists the supremacy of this plan. In our innermost being we are in the midst of this battle between Lucifer and the other beings. We are the arena for this battle. This draws us into karma, but only indirectly through the fact that this battle with Lucifer is taking place. On the other hand, when we look toward the outside, we are drawn into ahrimanic powers. What then takes place comes from outside, and this is where Ahriman enters us.

Now, we know that there were beings on the Old Moon who were going through their human stage at that time, similar to what we are doing in the course of Earth's evolution. In *Cosmic Memory*[2] and in *An Outline of Occult Science*,[3] you find these beings described as angels, angeloi, or dhyanis, but the names are not important. At that time, a fight was going on within these beings that was similar to the luciferic fight within our own being. On the Old Moon these beings were the arena of a battle taking place because of those beings who had lagged behind on the Sun. This battle on Old Moon had nothing to do with our inner I, because

---

2. Rudolf Steiner, *Cosmic Memory: Prehistory of Earth and Man*, Steinerbooks, Blauvelt, NY, 1987.
3. Rudolf Steiner, *An Outline of Occult Science*, Anthroposophic Press, Hudson, NY, 1972. These two books also describe in great detail the planetary stages of human and cosmic evolution referred to by Steiner in this lecture. These stages of evolution are referred to by planetary names, but are only indirectly related to the physical planets in our solar system.

on the Moon human beings did not yet possess an I. It took place outside what our I could be involved in; it took place on the Old Moon "in the bosom of the angels." As a result, these beings developed in a way only possible because of the influence of the beings who lagged behind during the Sun evolution. Those beings played a role for the angeloi that corresponds to the role luciferic beings now play for us. The beings held back during the Sun evolution are the ahrimanic beings; the beings that were held back during the Moon evolution are the luciferic beings. This is why we can only approach ahrimanic beings indirectly. But it was Ahriman who was the tempter in the bosom of the angeloi, so to speak. Ahriman was at work in them, and through him the angeloi became what they became and carried it along with them, just as they brought along their good accomplishments.

The good thing that we receive from Lucifer is the ability to distinguish between good and evil, to make free decisions, to achieve free will. For us, this can only be achieved through Lucifer. The angelic beings, however, have accomplished something that they now bring along into earthly existence. We can describe this by saying that the angeloi, now surrounding us as spiritual beings, prepared themselves for their present existence by means of the ahrimanic battle in their souls during the Old Moon's evolution. What these beings have experienced and the effect it has had on them is not a concern for our innermost I; we are not involved in it with our I. (We will see how we come indirectly to this—again because of ahrimanic influence in us.) What these beings achieved under ahrimanic influence was the result of causes they had assimilated during their Moon existence. This was then carried over into our Earth existence. Let us try to discover what emerges in our Earth existence as one such effect of this earlier ahrimanic battle.

If this ahrimanic battle on Old Moon had not taken place, these beings would not have been able to carry into our Earth existence what had belonged to Old Moon existence. It would have ended when the Old Moon perished. But because the angeloi absorbed the ahrimanic influence, they have become entangled in Moon existence, just as we become entangled in Earth existence through luciferic influence. They took the Moon element into their inmost being and carried it over into our Earth existence. As a result, they are able to call forth what must be present within Earth existence if our Earth is not to succumb wholly to the influence of Lucifer. Our Earth as a whole would have to succumb to the influence of Lucifer if the conditions relating to the angels' battle with Ahriman on Old Moon had not been carried into our Earth existence.

What are the processes in our Earth existence that can be characterized as normal? When our present solar system was being organized to correspond to the goals of the Earth, what we see as the regular movements of the sun, the Earth, and the other planets appeared, causing day and night, the regular sequence of the seasons, sunshine and rain, flourishing crops in the fields, and so on. These are arrangements that are repeated continually according to the cosmic rhythm developed especially for this present Earth existence, now that Old Moon existence has sunk into obscurity. However, Lucifer is at work within Earth existence. We will see that he works in many situations besides where we can trace his activity in human beings themselves, although it is true that he has chosen this as his most important arena. But even if Lucifer were present only within earthly existence outside of us, we human beings would still fall into what we can call the luciferic temptation, simply through the ordered arrangements and regular courses of the planets around the sun, through the alternation of summer and winter, rain and sunshine, and so on. Simply through everything that can come to us from the structured cosmos, through everything brought about by the regular rhythmic movements of the solar system, we would have to succumb to the luciferic influence if the only laws in effect were those suited to the current universe. We would have to prefer a comfortable life to the task of winning our cosmic salvation; we would have to prefer the regular course of events to what we are supposed to accomplish through struggle.

For this reason, counter-forces had to be created. These counterforces came about through certain processes, highly beneficial and normal on Old Moon, that intervened in the regular cosmic processes of our life on Earth. When these processes work on Earth existence today, however, they are abnormal and endanger Earth's regular course. But when they appear, they exert a corrective influence, so to speak, on the tendency toward living in luxury, toward comfort and opulence, that would come about if cosmic rhythms alone were present. We see these forces at work in a violent hailstorm, for example. When something is destroyed that would have otherwise been created under the influence of the regular forces of Earth, the corrective is being exercised with an overall positive effect, even if we cannot acknowledge this to begin with. There is a higher reasoning than we human beings understand.

When a hailstorm flattens the fields, we can say that the forces storming in with the hail were once benevolent forces on the Old Moon, just as the forces blessing us with rain and sunshine have a beneficial effect today. Today the older forces come storming in to correct what luciferic influence would otherwise bring about. And if the ordered course of existence nevertheless continues, these forces come storming in all the more strongly in order to bring about an even greater degree of correction. Everything that leads to regular, progressive development belongs to the forces of Earth itself. When a volcano erupts lava, the forces that are at work in it are Old Moon forces that had been held back, but have been carried over from Old Moon in order to exert a corrective influence on our life on Earth. It is the same with earthquakes and all other natural disasters. We can realize that in the course of development as a whole, there actually is a rational basis for much of what comes from outside. It still remains for us to see what this has to do with human I-consciousness.

However, we must be clear about one thing: namely that all of these things represent only one side of human existence, of Earth existence, and of cosmic existence as such. We have said on the one hand that when an organ is destroyed, this is due to the benevolent effects of spiritual forces. We have also found that the entire course of the Earth's evolution must be corrected by forces from the Old Moon existence. We must now ask: How is it that we as earthly human beings must work to correct the harmful influences of Old Moon forces? We may suspect that as earthly human beings, we are not really allowed to go around wishing for volcanic eruptions and earthquakes; that we should not destroy organs ourselves in order to support the beneficial effect of the spiritual powers. But we can realize, with some justification, that if an epidemic breaks out somewhere, this happens to bring about something that people are actively seeking as a balance to something within themselves. We can assume that we are driven into certain circumstances to experience injury and, through overcoming it, move closer to a state of perfection.

So, what about hygienic and sanitary regulations? Wouldn't it be possible for someone to say: Since epidemics can have a very positive effect, it must be wrong to take all kinds of steps to promote public health, or take measures to prevent disease, because that would reduce the possibility of this positive effect coming about. Someone might well come to the conclusion that we should do nothing to reduce the impact of natural disasters, justifying this by saying that it is wholly in line with what was contained in the lectures yesterday and today.

We will see that this is not the case, or rather that it is not the case under certain circumstances. Now we are properly prepared to actually understand how benevolent influences can inflict damage on one of our organs so that we don't succumb to the effect of *maya*; only now are we ready to become conscious of the effect we call forth when we evade the results of these benevolent influences by taking sanitary and hygienic measures against disease. We are now at a point where we human beings often find ourselves: When an apparent contradiction appears and puts its whole force behind us, we are close to the point where ahrimanic powers can exert great influence on us. Nowhere is the possibility of submitting to illusions greater than when we are driven into a bottleneck like this. It is good that we have come to this point, because we can now say that the powers that make an organ unusable are benevolent ones, because this comes about as an effect to counter Ahriman. Therefore those who do not support what we can call "benevolent effects to counteract ahrimanic powers" are working to the detriment of humankind, because by taking hygienic measures and so on, we restrict this benevolent counter-effect.

We are in a bottleneck. It is good that we have been led into this contradiction so that we can consider that such contradictions are indeed possible, and can even be a good schooling for our spirit. Then, once we have seen how to rescue ourselves from this contradiction, we will have done something from within ourselves that can give us the strength to evade the deceptions of Ahriman.[4]

---

4. For more on karma in relation to natural events, see: Rudolf Steiner, *Karmic Relationships: Esoteric Studies*, vol. 2, Rudolf Steiner Press, London, 1974, lecture June 29, 1924.

3

Death and Birth in Relation to Karma

HAMBURG, MAY 26, 1910

As I have repeatedly commented, it will only be possible to sketch the great laws of karma in a few strokes, as a stimulus for our thinking in this infinitely broad area. If you think about everything we have talked about in the last few days, you will no longer find it remarkable that at certain levels of consciousness, people are actively driven to search in the outer world for effects that balance karmic causes they have incorporated into themselves. In searching for the consequence that will balance out a karmic cause they have taken in, people can be actively driven to contract an infection, for example. It is even possible for people to be driven toward so-called accidents in their life in order to attempt a balance through these occurrences.

But what happens to the course of karma when, through certain measures we've taken, we are in a position to prevent people from seeking balance in this way?

Let's assume that certain sanitary precautions we have taken make it impossible for certain causes to exist, and totally prevent some specific things that people must necessarily tend toward as a result of their karmic connections. Let's suppose that as a result of hygienic measures, certain pathogens are effectively combated in a particular area. We have already seen inwardly that it is not in people's best interest to take such measures. We saw, for example, that the predilection for sanitation laws, having disappeared for a time, reappears at another time simply because of inverse repetition in evolution. This led us to realize that people's decision to take such measures at a certain time in history lies well within the great laws of human karma. However, it will also be easy for us to understand why people in earlier ages did not get around to taking such measures: At an earlier point in time, humanity *needed* the epidemics that are now supposed to be done away with through preventive measures. With regard to life's major developments, human evolution really is subject to very specific laws. Measures such as these do not come from the fully conscious, rational, understandable life we call our own between birth and death, but from the spirit of humanity as a whole, so it is impossible to take such measures until they can be of use and significance for the evolution of humanity as a whole. You only need to keep in mind how some invention or discovery appears on the scene only when humankind is really ready for it. A brief overview of the history of human evolution on Earth has much to offer in this respect.

Think of how our ancestors—that is, our own souls—lived on the ancient continent of Atlantis. They lived in bodies that were totally different in form from modern human bodies. Then the Atlantean continent sank, and the developments we are undergoing today began to take place on our present continents. At a very particular point in time, the inhabitants of one newly emerged hemisphere were brought together with the inhabitants of the other for the first time. It was only a short time ago, in the not-so-distant past, that the peoples of Europe were once again able to reach the areas that had been separated from them on the other side of the Atlantean continent. Truly great laws govern these things. And whether certain discoveries are made, or certain measures taken that determine the possible direction of karmic intervention is independent of arbitrary human actions or opinions. These things take place when they are meant to take place. Regardless of this, when we do away with certain causes that otherwise would have been present for certain people to seek out through their karmic entanglements, we can indeed influence people's karma. We can influence it, but we cannot do away with it. We can only point karma in another direction.

Let's imagine a case in which a number of people feel compelled to seek out certain influences as karmic compensation. Meanwhile, however, these influences or circumstances have been done away with by means of sanitary precautions, and can no longer be found. But this does not free these people from what is demanded of them as a karmic consequence. On the contrary, they are compelled to seek other consequences. People do not escape their karma. That such precautionary measures have been taken does not relieve them of the burden of what they would otherwise have sought out.

You can infer from this that if we were in a position to do away with a karmic compensation, this would have to be compensated for in some other direction. By doing away with one influence or another, we only create the need to seek other opportunities and influences. Let us now assume that many epidemics or common causes of illness can simply be traced back to the fact that the people who seek the causes of illness are trying to do away with what they have instilled in themselves karmically—for example, a predisposition to unkindness or lack of love in the case of a smallpox epidemic. Even if we managed to get rid of this predisposition, the cause of the lovelessness would still persist, and the souls in question would then have to find appropriate compensation in a different way, either in this incarnation or in another one. We can grasp what is taking place here when we point to something inevitable.

It is a fact these days that many outer influences and causes are being done away with. We are getting rid of what would otherwise have been sought out in order to balance out specific karmic burdens taken up by humanity in earlier times. By doing so, we are only doing away with the possibility of people succumbing to outer influences. We make their outer life healthier or more pleasant. But all we accomplish by doing this is to make them find a different way of seeking the karmic balance they would otherwise have found through the appropriate illness. The souls that are rescued nowadays in this way with regard to their health are condemned to seek this karmic balance in other ways. They are forced to look for it in many of the cases described here. Healthier living makes their physical existence more advantageous and their physical life easier, but the soul is influenced in the opposite way. It will gradually begin to experience a certain emptiness, dissatisfaction or lack of fulfillment. If outer life were to continue getting more pleasant and healthy, as is generally thought possible from living in a purely materialistic way, then such souls would have less and less incentive to make progress within themselves. Parallel to this, the soul would begin to stultify in a certain sense.

This is already noticeable to anyone looking at life more closely. More than in almost any other age, people today live in pleasant circumstances but go around with vacant, uninvolved souls. This is why people hurry from one sensation to the next. Then, if finances permit, they travel from place to place to see something else, or if forced to stay in the same place, they spend every evening hurrying from one amusement to the next. In spite of all that, however, their souls remain vacant. In the end they no longer know what to look for in order to acquire any content at all. Living in purely outward, physically pleasant circumstances creates the tendency in people to think only about physical things. If this tendency to occupy oneself only with the physical had not been around for so long, the tendency toward theoretical materialism would also not be as strong as it is now. Our souls suffer more, while our outer life is made healthier.

Theosophists have the least reason to complain about this state of affairs, because theosophy brings about an understanding of things wherever it works, and thus creates insight into the basis of balance. Souls can remain empty only up to a certain point, and then they snap over to the other side as a result of their own elasticity, as it were. They then look for a content that is related to their own depths, and realize how great their need is to achieve a theosophical worldview.

So we see that while the effects of materialistic views on life may well make outer life easier, they create difficulties for the inner life that then lead, as a result of the soul's suffering, to search for the content of a spiritual worldview. The spiritual worldview that announces itself today as the theosophical view thus comes to meet those souls who cannot find satisfaction in desolation, in the impressions that outer life, no matter how pleasantly arranged, can offer them. These souls will go on seeking and constantly taking in new things until their elasticity works so strongly from the other side that they then unite themselves with what we may call "spiritual life." Thus a relationship exists between sanitation and the hopes of the spiritual-scientific worldview for the future.

You can already notice this on a small scale. Nowadays there are certain souls who add a superficial interest in the theosophical worldview to all their other superficialities, souls who take up the theosophical worldview as a new sensation. This is evident in every current in human evolution: Anything that is of profound inner significance also has an effect as a fad, as a sensation. But the souls who are truly prepared for theosophy are either those who feel dissatisfied with outer sensations or those who realize that all the explanations of superficial science cannot explain the actual facts. These are the people whose overall karma has prepared them to be able to unite the most intimate aspects of their soul life with theosophy. Spiritual science also belongs to the karma of humanity as a whole, and will thus find its place in it.

As we have seen, we can make people's karma take a different direction, but we cannot prevent it from working back on them. What a person has prepared for him or herself in the course of previous lifetimes will always come back in one way or another.

We can best show how karma can have a meaningful effect in the world by considering an example in which karma works without moral overtones, where it works in the greater world without having anything to do with what people develop out of their own souls as moral impulses that then lead to moral or immoral actions. Let's present our souls with an aspect of karma in which morality plays no role as yet, where something neutral constitutes the karmic interconnection.

Let's assume there is a woman living in a particular incarnation. Surely you will not question the fact that this woman, simply because she is a woman, will necessarily have different experiences than a man has. These experiences are related not only to inner soul processes, but also to a very great extent to outer events, to circumstances in which she finds herself only because she is a woman. These circumstances, in turn, work back on her entire constitution and mood of soul. We can thus talk about how a woman is led to certain actions that are intimately connected to her being female. As we know, it is only in the domain of spiritual interaction that it makes no difference whether a person is male or female. The more deeply we descend into what is merely soul and into the outer aspect of the human being, the greater the difference becomes between the lives of a man and a woman. So we can say that a woman also differs from a man in certain soul qualities, tending more toward those qualities that lead to impulses characterized as emotional impulses. She is better endowed than a man when it comes to having soul experiences. In the life of a man, intellectualism and materialism—which came to us through men, after all—are more at home. This has a great influence on a man's soul life. By their very natures, a woman is predestined more to psychological and emotional factors, and a man to intellectual and materialistic ones. Thus, certain nuances are present in the soul life of a woman simply because she is a woman.

Now, we have described how what we experience as soul qualities between death and rebirth penetrates the organic structure of our next body. Our more strongly psychological and emotional aspect, which tends toward the inner part of the soul during life between birth and death, also has the tendency to intervene more deeply in our bodily organization, impregnating it much more intensely. Because a woman assimilates impressions related to this psychological and emotional aspect, she also takes her life experiences into the deeper foundations of her soul. A man's experiences may be richer and more scientific, but they do not go as deeply into his soul life as is the case with a woman. In a woman, the whole world of her experiences imprints itself deeply on the soul. Because of this, her experiences tend to work into the organic structure of the body more deeply and embrace it more strongly in the future. Thus, a female incarnation acquires the tendency to reach deeply into the structure of the body through the experiences of one incarnation, and therefore to shape the body itself in the next incarnation. However, to work deeply into the body, to penetrate the body thoroughly, means to produce a male organism. A male organism is brought forth by the forces of the soul wanting to make a deeper impression on the material aspect. So, you can see that experiences as a woman in one incarnation produce a male organism in the next incarnation. The very nature of esoteric work supplies you with a relationship that transcends morality. This is why esoteric teachings say that the man is the karma of the woman. In fact, a male body in a later incarnation is the result of experiences in a preceding incarnation as a woman. At the risk of arousing the antagonism of some of those present—there are always modern men who have an unholy fear of incarnating as a woman—I must once again shed objective light on this matter.

Now, what about a man's experiences? In the case of a man's experiences, we will understand them best by taking what we have just presented as our starting point. In the male body, the inner human being lives its way into matter more fundamentally, embracing it more completely than does a woman. A woman retains more of her spiritual aspect in an unembodied state; she does not enter as deeply into matter, and her bodily nature remains softer. She does not separate herself from the spiritual to such a great extent. The female nature characteristically retains more free spirituality, working less deeply into matter. Above all, it keeps the brain more flexible. Therefore, it is not surprising that women have a special predilection for new things, especially in spiritual fields, because they have kept their spiritual aspect freer. It presents less resistance. It isn't by chance, but corresponds to a profound law, that more women than men find their way to any movement that is spiritual in nature. Any man knows what a difficult tool the male brain often is. It presents terrible obstacles when you try to use it for a flexible train of thought; it simply does not want to go along with it. It must first be educated through all possible means in order to free itself from this inflexibility. It is quite possible for a man to experience this personally.

A man's nature, therefore, is more condensed and contracted; it has been pressed together more, and made stiffer and harder by the inner human being. It is more materialized. Now, a less flexible brain is primarily a suitable tool for the intellect, but less so for the psyche, since the intellect is something that relates much more to the physical plane. What can be characterized as male intellectualism comes from the man's stiffer, densified brain. We could even speak of the male brain as being "frozen" to a certain extent. It must first thaw out if it is to find its way into more subtle trains of thought. This causes a man to grasp more of the external world, but less of the experiences within the depths of soul life. What he takes up does not go very deep, either. An outer proof of this is how little ordinary science goes into depth, and how little it grasps the inner aspect of things. To be sure, it includes the broader context in its thinking, but it does not bring the facts together thoroughly. Conventional science unhesitatingly allows a parallel and separate existence for some things. This is enough to nauseate anyone whose self-discipline requires that facts be brought into connection. You can see how little these things go into depth.

Here is one example of how superficial things can be in modern science: Assume that some young person is a student in a university department where some rabid Darwinist is a lecturer. From this person who represents the theory of natural selection, the student hears how a rooster's feathers come to have such a beautiful iridescent blue coloration. This is traced back to sexual selectivity, because the rooster attracts hens with this blue color, and the hens select the roosters with iridescent blue feathers. Meanwhile the other roosters get short-changed, and as a result this particular variety of poultry develops. This is higher evolution: *sexual selectivity*!

The student, pleased at having learned how evolution can progress, goes on to a class in another department where, let us say, they are discussing sense physiology. It might happen in this second department that the student hears the following: Experiments have been made showing how the colors of the spectrum affect various animals differently. It can be proved, for example, that chickens do not perceive that part of the spectrum including blue and purple, but only the part extending from green through orange to red and infrared!

Now if the student is to reconcile these two facts (which can actually be heard nowadays), things must be taken superficially. The whole theory of natural selection rests on the supposition that the hens see something pleasurable in the cock's bright colors, whereas in fact they cannot see these colors at all; they are coal-black for a hen.

This is just one example. But these are the kinds of things that are met with everywhere by those who really want to research things scientifically. And you can see from this that intellectuality does not penetrate very deeply into life, but remains on the surface. I have deliberately chosen crass examples.

We will be reluctant to believe that intellectuality is something that runs its course in a fairly superficial way, does not penetrate deeply into our soul life, and does little to grasp the inner aspect of the human being. But a materialistic point of view, in particular, does not comprehend our soul life. As a result, however, if a person does not work deeply into the soul during this incarnation, this person acquires the tendency to penetrate less deeply into the bodily organization in the next incarnation. This person has acquired less strength to do so, and as a result, penetrates bodily existence less deeply. This, however, brings about the tendency to build up a female body in the next incarnation. Once again, it is true when it is said in esoteric teachings that the woman is the man's karma.

In this morally neutral field, we have seen that what people prepare for themselves in one incarnation organizes their bodily existence in the next. These things not only penetrate deeply into our inner life, but also into our outer experiences and actions. Therefore, we must say that when a person has the experiences of a man or of a woman in one incarnation, that person's outer actions in the next incarnation are determined, in one way or another—through having had a woman's experiences, which tends to build up a male body, or through having had a man's experiences, which tends to build up a female body. Only in rare instances does an individual have the same sex in successive incarnations, and this can repeat no more than seven times. As a rule, however, a male body strives to become female in the next incarnation and vice versa. No resistance on our part will make any difference, because it doesn't depend on what we want in the physical world, but rather on our inclinations in the time between death and rebirth. These inclinations are determined by reasons more rational than the horror, for example, that a person going through a male incarnation may have at the thought of incarnating as a woman in his next life. Thus you can see how our later life is karmically determined by our earlier life, and how our actions in a later life can also be predetermined.

Next, we need to learn to recognize another karmic connection, one that is essential to the illumination of some important things to be considered during the next few days.

Let's look back in time to a very distant point in human evolution, when human incarnations on Earth first began. This took place in ancient Lemurian times. The important thing to consider about that time is that first the luciferic influence worked on human beings in a far-reaching manner, and this then called forth the ahrimanic influence. Let us attempt to place before our souls how the luciferic influence worked outwardly in human life. Simply because human beings in those ancient times acquired the capacity to take up the luciferic influence—that is, because they could allow their astral bodies to be pervaded with the luciferic influence—their astral bodies became inclined to penetrate much more deeply into the physical body's organization, to descend into its material aspect, and to make this descent in a very different way than would have been the case without the luciferic influence. Through the luciferic influence, human beings became much more material. Without the working of the luciferic influence, human beings would have acquired less tendency to descend into the material world and would have remained in higher regions of existence. So a much stronger penetration of the outer and inner human being took place than would have been the case without the luciferic influence.

Because they were more strongly bound up with the material aspect of the outer body, people lost the possibility of looking back on events preceding their incarnation. Human beings now entered existence through a sort of birth that united them deeply with matter and erased any possibility of looking back on earlier events. Otherwise, people would have preserved the memory of what they had experienced in the spirit before birth. Through the luciferic influence, birth now became an act through which we brought about such intense connections between the outer and inner human being that our earlier experience in the spiritual world was wiped out. Human beings were robbed of their memories of earlier spiritual events. Being bound to outer bodily existence eliminated the possibility for people to look back on earlier events. This meant that during each lifetime people were obliged to draw only on the outer world for their experiences.

Now, one would really be on the wrong track to believe that only the crude outer substances we take in can affect us. What works on us includes not only the nourishing substances and forces we take in, but also other experiences we have, such as what flows into us through our senses. But because of the coarser connection to matter that has come about, even the substances that nourish us work differently. Imagine that the luciferic influence were not there. In that case, everything from nutrients to sense impressions would have a much more subtle effect on us. Everything we experience as interaction with the outer world would be permeated by what we experienced between death and rebirth.

But because we have given our material aspect a denser configuration, we also tend to take up denser things.

The effect of the luciferic influence, is that we have made matter more dense, and therefore draw much denser substance toward us from the outer world than we would have otherwise. The denser substance we now draw toward us is totally different from something less dense, which would have maintained our memories of earlier life, and also would have made us certain that everything we live through between birth and death has consequences that go on forever. We would know that although death occurs outwardly, everything that has happened goes on working. But because of having to take in denser substance, we create a strong interaction between our own bodily nature and the external world, an interaction that begins at birth.

What is the consequence of this interaction? The spiritual world has been extinguished for us at birth. And before we can live in the spirit, before we can wake up in the spiritual world, everything that comes into us from outside as denser materiality must have been taken away from us again. Having acquired a denser materiality, we must now wait for outer material bodily existence to be taken from us if we are to enter the spirit once again. Beginning at birth, the denser materiality that penetrates us destroys our human bodily existence bit by bit. What flows into us in this way destroys our bodily existence more and more, to the point where it can no longer persist. Starting at birth, we take in a denser materiality than we would have without the luciferic influence. As a result, we slowly destroy our bodily nature until it becomes totally unusable and death follows.

So we see that the luciferic influence is the karmic cause of death for the human being. If birth did not exist in this form, death would also not exist in this form. We would face death with a secure view of things to come. Death is the karmic consequence of birth; birth and death are karmically related. Without birth as we now live through it, there would also be no death as we now live through it.

I have already said that we cannot speak of karma with regard to animals in the same sense as we do regarding human beings. Someone who says that an animal's birth and death are also karmically related does not know that birth and death for a human being are totally different than for an animal. Although outwardly they appear similar, inwardly they are not the same at all. What is important about birth and death is not built up outwardly, but is undergone inwardly. In the case of animals, only the species soul, the group soul, has experiences. For the group soul, the significance of an individual animal's death is about the same as the experience of getting your hair cut shorter in the summer and letting it slowly grow back. The group soul of an animal species experiences the death of a single animal as the dying-off of a member that is gradually replaced. Thus the group soul is what we may compare to the human I. It does not know birth and death; it constantly looks back to what precedes birth and forward to what follows death. It is nonsense to speak of the birth and death of animals in the same way we do concerning human beings, because they are preceded by totally different causes. And we deny the inner effectiveness of the spirit when we believe that what seems outwardly similar is necessarily brought about by inwardly similar causes. Similarity of outer processes never points with certainty to similar causes. The causes that underlie human birth are totally different from those underlying animal birth; humans and animals also die because of totally different causes.

If we were to think a bit about how similar external appearances can be without the inner experience being even remotely similar, we would arrive at this understanding purely methodologically. There is a very simple way of coming to the conclusion that outer sensory appearances are no indicator of inner activity. Imagine two people. You arrive at a certain place at nine o'clock and see these two people standing next to each other. At three o'clock, not having been there in the meantime, you again pass the same spot. The two people are standing there again. You could conclude that person A is still standing in the same place, and B is also still standing just where he was at nine o'clock. However, if you investigate what these people have been doing meanwhile, you may find out that one of them has actually remained standing there, while the other has gone for a long walk and gotten tired. Their presence there is based on quite different processes. It would be ridiculous to say that because they are both standing in the same place again at three o'clock, the same things must have gone on inside them. It would be just as ridiculous to find two similarly shaped cells and to conclude from their similar structure that they have the same significance inwardly. The important thing is to know the entire factual context that has led each cell to the place in question. This is why modern cell physiology, which proceeds from the investigation of inner cellular structure, is on the wrong track. What presents itself to outer sensory observation can never be conclusive with regard to the inner nature of things.

We must think things through in this manner if we want to achieve insight into what is revealed to spiritual scientists through esoteric observations, such as how birth and death are completely different for a human being than for a mammal or a bird. It will only be possible to study these things when people once again adopt a little of what spiritual research has to say. Until then, outer science, which stops short at sensory appearances and outer facts, will be able to bring very nice facts to light, but under these circumstances people's opinions about these facts will never correspond to reality. That is why all of today's theoretical science is an illusory structure that has come about through combining outer facts according to outer appearances. In some fields, the outer facts even beg to be interpreted in the right way, but our current opinions prevent us from doing it.

Today we have let ourselves be touched by two neutral areas in the field of karmic law, and you will see how they can be a foundation for our further considerations. We have seen how the female body is the karmic consequence of male experiences and the male body the karmic consequence of female experiences.

And at the end, we also saw that in human life, death is a karmic consequence of birth. This is something that, if we gradually try to understand it, can lead us deeply into karmic connections in human life.[1]

---

1. For further reading on the effects of karma on soul qualities: Rudolf Steiner, *Karmic Relationships: Esoteric Studies,* vol. 5, Rudolf Steiner Press, London, 1966, lecture March 30, 1924.

4

Knowledge of Reincarnation and Karma through Thought-Exercises

STUTTGART, FEBRUARY 20, 1912

If we take into account life going on around us, casting its waves into our inner being, so to speak, and into everything that we ourselves must perceive, suffer, or enjoy during physical existence on Earth, we can contemplate several distinct groups or types of experience.

To begin with, if we look more at ourselves and what lies within our abilities and talents, we will find that when we succeed at something or other, we can say to ourselves, "Well, given the kind of person you are, it is very natural and understandable that you should succeed at this particular thing." On the other hand, when we meet with failure in certain instances, with what we call "bad luck" because we did not succeed, this may also seem quite understandable in the total context of our being.

In such cases, we may not always be able to demonstrate exactly how a certain bad luck—something we have not succeeded at—is related to our inability in some particular direction. But even though we may not see a direct connection between our failure and any inability on our part, if in general we must say to ourselves, "You know, in many respects you really have been frivolous in this earthly life; it's quite conceivable that you deserved this lack of success," then we can also understand on a general level that it was not possible for everything to proceed like clockwork if we were being frivolous.

From what has just been discussed, you might think that we ought to be able to recognize a causal relationship of a sort to what must necessarily happen as a result of our own abilities and inabilities. But with many things in life, no matter how precisely we proceed, we don't manage to relate our success or lack of it to our abilities or inabilities in any direct way. In these instances, it remains obscure to us how we were to blame for something or how we deserved it. In short, when we contemplate our inner life, we can distinguish two groups of experiences. With the first group, we are conscious of how things relate to the causes of our success or failure; with the second, we cannot see any such connection. In this latter case, it seems more or less chance that we fail at one thing and succeed at another. For the time being, let's simply note that this second group of facts and experiences does indeed exist. We will turn our attention to it later.

In contrast to what has just been discussed, let's now turn our attention more toward our outer destiny. In this regard, we also need to consider two groups of phenomena. On the one hand, we can contemplate cases where we may recognize inwardly that with regard to events that come to meet us—*not* what we ourselves have undertaken—we ourselves have brought about certain things and are to blame for them. But with regard to another group, we will be very much inclined to say that we cannot see any connection to what we wanted or intended. In ordinary life, we usually say of such events that they entered our life as if by chance, apparently unrelated to anything we ourselves have brought about.

We will now consider with regard to our inner life this second group—that is, those events that we cannot recognize as directly related to our abilities and inabilities. These are the outer events that we call coincidental, that we cannot recognize as having been brought about by anything that went before.

We can do an experiment of a sort with these two groups of experiences. Doing the experiment does not commit us to anything, of course; we will only be trying out what will now be described.

We can do this experiment by imagining how it would be if we were to invent an imaginary person of some sort, a thought-up person whom we equip with the character traits and abilities needed to bring about precisely those incomprehensible things that we know are not related to our own abilities. Such a person, therefore, would be one whose abilities are such that he or she would necessarily succeed or fail at things that we cannot ascribe to our own abilities or inabilities. We imagine this person as someone who artificially and very deliberately brings about the things that seem to have entered our life by chance.

We can start with very simple examples in order to make this clear. Let's assume that a roofing tile has fallen on our shoulder and injured it. At first we will tend to say that this is chance. But now, as an experiment, let's invent an imaginary person who would do the following strange things: We invent a person who climbs up on the roof and quickly loosens a tile, but leaves it still hanging there. Then this imaginary person runs back down again quickly, just in time for the tile to fall on his or her shoulder. We then do the same thing for all seemingly coincidental events that have entered our life—we invent an imaginary person who is to blame for bringing about everything that we cannot recognize in ordinary life as having any connection to us.

To begin with, doing this can seem like merely playing with thoughts. We do not commit ourselves to anything by doing it, and yet, something remarkable begins to happen as we go along. Once we have thought up such a person and endowed him or her with the characteristics we have described, this artificial thought-person makes a very remarkable impression on us. We can no longer get away from the image we have made of this person, even though it seems to be such an artificial construction. It fascinates us; it gives the impression of having something to do with us after all. This is the result of the sensation we acquire from confronting this artificial thought-person. If we get deeply absorbed in this image, it will certainly never let go of us. A remarkable process begins to take place in our soul, a process we can compare to an inner soul process that people undergo at every moment: Thinking about something or making a decision may require something that we used to know, and we apply all kinds of artificial means in the attempt to remember it. In our efforts to recall something that has escaped our memory, we go through the process of "trying to remember," as we call it in everyday life. All the thoughts we use to help us in this attempt to remember are accessory thoughts. Just try to figure out how many of these accessory thoughts you often need to use and then let go of again to arrive at what you wanted to know! These accessory thoughts are there to clear the way for what we want to remember, for what we actually need at the moment.

The thought-person we have described is a similar accessory process, but much more comprehensive. It no longer lets us go; because of how it works in us, we can say that it lives in us as a thought. It is something that goes on working in us and undergoes a transformation in us. It actually transforms itself into an idea, a thought, that then appears in the same way as something recollected in the ordinary process of remembering, something that overwhelms us as it appears. It is as if something were saying, "This thought-person cannot remain the same, but changes within you, develops life, and becomes something different." This experience forces itself upon us—just try doing the experiment!—and tells us that this is something having to do with an earthly life that is not the same as our current one. This thought will most certainly appear, a kind of recollection of another earthly life. It is more a feeling or sensation than a thought, but it's as if we experience what appears in our soul as what we ourselves once were in an earlier incarnation on Earth.

If we look at anthroposophy as a whole, it is certainly not merely a sum-total of theories or communicated facts that exist for themselves. Rather, it gives us directions and indications as to how certain things are achieved. Anthroposophy states that if you do this or that, it will lead you to be able to recollect more easily. It can also be said (and this is taken from actual experience) that when you proceed as already described, you will feel an impression of the person you once were. With this, we arrive at what we might call an expansion of our capacity to recollect. To begin with, as long as we are actually constructing the thought-person described above, what opens up for us is really only a phenomenon of thought. But the thought-person does not remain a thought-person. It transforms itself into perceptual impressions, into felt impressions, and when it does, what we are feeling tells us that we are dealing with something having to do with our preceding incarnation. Our memory begins to extend to our earlier incarnation.

In our present incarnation we remember things if we have been present in them with our thoughts. You all know that it is relatively easy for us to remember things that have played into our thoughts. In ordinary life, however, it is not so easy to keep alive what played into our feelings. If you try to think back on what caused you great pain ten or twenty years ago, you will easily recall the mental image. You will make your way back through your mental images to what took place then, but you cannot go back to a living sensation of the pain you experienced. Pain subsides, and our recollection of it is poured out into the mental image.

What has been described is a feeling recollection. Indeed, this is how we come to feel our earlier incarnation. What appears can be called a recollection of earlier incarnations. But what plays into our current incarnation cannot simply be seen as the bearer of our memory of earlier incarnations. Just consider how intimately our concepts are connected with our means of expressing them, with our language. Language is the embodiment of the world of concepts. And every human being must learn language anew in each lifetime. Even the greatest linguists had to master their mother tongue with great effort when they were children. There have not yet been cases of students who easily learn Greek because they remember the Greek they spoke in an earlier incarnation!

The poet Hebbel once outlined some thoughts for a drama he wanted to write. It's unfortunate that he never wrote it, because it would have been a very interesting play. The plot consisted of Plato reincarnating as a student and getting the very worst grades for his explanations of the old Plato. It's too bad that Hebbel never carried out his plan. We need not attribute this simply to teachers' pedantry, and so on. We know that what Hebbel noted is based on the fact that our conceptual activity—what takes place in our direct conceptions of our experiences—is more or less limited to the present incarnation. And it is true that the first impression of our preceding incarnation appears directly as a new kind of recollection, as a feeling memory. The impression you have when this memory arises out of the thought-person you have constructed is more like a feeling, but a feeling that leads you to understand that this impression comes from some person who used to exist, and that person was you! As the first impression of our preceding incarnation, we get something like a feeling memory.

Constructing this thought-person as described above is only a means to an end. It then transforms itself into an impression or feeling. Anyone approaching anthroposophy will have the opportunity, more or less, to easily carry out what has been described. Having done so, they will find that they really do get an inner impression which, to use a different example, could be described like this: "I once saw a landscape, and although I have forgotten what it looked like, I know I liked it." Now if this took place in the present lifetime, the landscape will no longer make a very vivid impression on our feelings, but if the impression stems from a previous incarnation, the impression it makes on them will be particularly vivid. It is possible for us to get a particularly vivid impression of this sort as a feeling impression of our earlier incarnation. And if we then observe these impressions objectively, we will at times get a bitter, bittersweet, or sour sensation from what results from the transformation of this thought-person. This sensation, sweet-and-sour or whatever it may be, is a feeling impression, an emotional impression of a sort.

The attempt has been made to draw your attention to something that can call forth in each of us a direct experience of the certainty of having existed in earlier lifetimes. This certainty comes about through feeling—through acquiring felt or emotional impressions that we have certainly not acquired during this present lifetime. However, an impression of this sort appears in the same way that mental images of memory appear in our ordinary life. We may question how we can know that this impression is actually a memory, and it can only be said that things like this cannot be proved. However, this is the same as any other instance in life when we remember something and are sound of mind: We can know that what appears in thought actually relates to an experience. Our experience itself provides the certainty. And what we picture in the way already described also provides the certainty that the impression in our mind relates to something having to do with us, not in our present life, but in the preceding one.

By artificial means, we have thus called up something in ourselves that brings us into connection with our preceding life. There are many other kinds of experimental inner experiences we can undergo that will take us further toward waking up something like perceptions of earlier lives.

Then again, there is also another way of dividing our experiences in life, of separating them into groups. On one side, we can group together everything we have endured in the way of suffering, pain, and setbacks; on the other side, everything we have become aware of as advancements, pleasure, joy, and so on.

Once again, we can experimentally take the following point of view: We can say that we have experienced certain pain and suffering. For us as we are in this incarnation, in the normal course of life, suffering is something negative; we would like to fend it off in a certain respect. Let's experiment by not doing that. Let's assume experimentally that for some reason we ourselves have brought about suffering and setbacks because we have become less perfect through our actions in earlier lives—if in fact such lives existed. Not only do we become more perfect in the course of our incarnations, we also become less perfect in some respects. Aren't we less perfect when we have injured some other person or caused hardship for another? Not only have we done something to this person, we have also taken something away from ourselves. As an overall personality, we would have been worth more had we not done that. We have a record of many such things, things we have done that are the basis of our imperfection. But what needs to happen if we have wronged someone and want to reestablish our worth? We must balance the wrongdoing, bring a compensatory action into the world; we must invent a means that forces us to overcome something, so to speak. If we can think along these lines about our pain and suffering, we will often realize that this pain and suffering, if overcome, are well suited to give us the strength we need to overcome our imperfections. We can become more perfect through our suffering.

This is not how we think in ordinary human life where we relate negatively to suffering. It can be said, however, that all pain and suffering, every obstacle in life, is intended to indicate that there is a person inside us who is more sensible than we are ourselves. For the moment, let's imagine the person who is, who encompasses the person's consciousness as the less sensible one. However, we do have a more sensible person slumbering in the depths of our soul. With our usual consciousness, we relate negatively to pain and suffering, but this more sensible person leads us to this very pain in spite of our consciousness, because we will be able to get rid of something through overcoming the pain. This person leads us to pain and suffering, instructs us to undergo it.

This may be a difficult thought to begin with, but thinking it does not commit us to anything; we can do it simply as an experiment. We can say that there is a more sensible person inside us who leads us to suffering and pain, to things we would consciously prefer to avoid. We will think of this person in us as the more sensible one. In this way, we arrive at the conclusion, disturbing to many, that the more sensible person in us always leads us to things we do not like! Therefore, let's assume the existence of this more sensible person who leads us to things we do not like so that we can make progress.

There is still something else we shall do, however. Let's take our pleasures, joys, and advancements and—just as an experiment—ask ourselves how it would be if we were to imagine, regardless of how things actually are, that we have not earned these joys, pleasures, and advancements, but that they have come to us through the grace of higher spiritual powers? This need not always be the case, but we will assume experimentally that we have brought about all our own pain and suffering, that the more sensible person inside us has led us to them because we recognize that we need them as a consequence of our imperfections, which we can only overcome through pain and suffering. And then we will also experimentally assume the opposite, and not attribute our joys to our having earned them, but will assume that they have been given to us by spiritual powers.

Again, thinking this way may be a bitter pill for some conceited people to swallow. However, if we undertake this as an experiment and are capable of intense imagination, it is certainly something self-transforming and self-corrective, to the extent that we were mistaken to begin with. It will lead to the fundamental perception that something lives in us that has nothing to do with our ordinary consciousness, and which is actually more profound than anything we have consciously experienced in this lifetime. In other words, something is present in us that is like a more sensible person who gladly turns to the eternal, divine, spiritual powers that live in and animate the world. Then, in our inner life, we become certain of a higher inner individuality existing behind the outer one. Through thought exercises such as these, we become aware of the eternal spiritual core of our being. This is extraordinarily significant. And once again, this is something we can actually *do*.

In every respect, anthroposophy can point the way for us not only to know something of the existence of another world, but to feel ourselves as members of this other world, as individualities who go through successive incarnations.

There is still a third type of experience. However, this will be more difficult to use, as it were, to really come to a sort of inner experience of karma and reincarnation. But although it is slow and difficult, what I will now relate can also be applied experimentally. And if it is conscientiously applied to our outer life, we will discover—first as a probability that we can believe in, but then with ever greater certainty—that this really is how our present life connects to the preceding one.

Let's assume that we are going through our current life between birth and death, and that we are in our thirties or older. (As we shall see, those who are not yet so far on in years will have the corresponding experiences later.) Consider how, in our thirties, we were led into contact with certain people in the outer world. It will seem evident to us that the connections made during that time came about when we were most ready for life and most fully present as mature individuals. This is something that can become clear if we reflect on it. In addition, reflection gained from a knowledge of spiritual science, from its basic principles, can lead us to the truth of what I have just said—even though this was communicated not only on the basis of such reflections, but also on the basis of spiritual-scientific research. That is, what I am now saying has not only been found to be logical through thinking, but has also been determined through spiritual-scientific research. Logical thinking can consolidate the facts, however, and confirm that they make sense.

If we think like this about many things we have learned, such as how the different individual members of a human being unfold in the course of life—we know how the ether body appears in the seventh year, the astral body in the fourteenth year, the sentient soul in the twenty-first year, the mind soul in the twenty-eighth year, and the consciousness soul in the thirty-fifth—if we think about this, we recognize that between the ages of thirty and forty we are involved with the development of the mind soul and the consciousness soul.

The mind and consciousness souls are those forces in human nature that lead us together most intimately with the outer physical world. These forces are intended to be especially pronounced in the stage of life when we are most involved with the outer physical world. During the first stage of childhood, the forces of our physical body are caused, directed, and determined by what is still contained within. At that stage, whatever causal factors we have acquired in previous incarnations, whatever has gone with us through the gate of death, whatever spiritual forces we have gathered, and whatever we bring along from our earlier life—all of this lives and works to build up our physical body. It works constantly and invisibly into the body from the inside outward. As we get older, this effect increasingly diminishes as the time of life approaches when the old forces have finished making the body. Then the time comes when we face the world with a completed organism; what we carry within us has been expressed in our outer body.

Around age thirty—perhaps somewhat earlier or later—we are most physical in confronting the world; in our relationship with it, we are then most closely related to the physical plane. We may then believe that we possess the utmost clarity—outer physical clarity—regarding the circumstances of life we then enter, but we must realize that of all those circumstances we will encounter in this incarnation, these are the least connected to what has been living and working most deeply within us since our birth. And yet we can assume that it is not by chance that we are brought together with the people who necessarily appear in our surroundings when we are around thirty years old. On the contrary, we can assume that our karma is also at work in us, and that these people also have something to do with one of our earlier incarnations.

Spiritual-scientific facts, researched in various ways, show that the people with whom we come together around age thirty usually had a connection to us at the beginning of, or even prior to, the preceding incarnation, as parents or siblings. Now, this is a strange and surprising situation. It doesn't always have to be like this, of course, but spiritual research shows that this is indeed the case in many instances. Our parents—who were with us at the beginning of our preceding lifetime and from whom we later separated—are karmically linked to us in such a way that they are brought together with us again in our current life—not during our childhood, but only when we have most completely entered the physical plane. It does not invariably happen like this. Spiritual-scientific research often shows that we only encounter the people who presently surround us during our thirties in a still later incarnation as parents, siblings, or other blood relatives. In other words, the people with whom we become acquainted during our thirties in any given incarnation are related to us by blood, either in the incarnation before that or the one that follows. So, we can say that the people we come together with during our thirties were either with us as parents and siblings in a preceding incarnation, or we can assume that this will be their relationship to us in a later incarnation.

The reverse is also true. Consider the people we have the least choice about, in terms of voluntarily choosing them by means of outer forces adapted to the physical plane—our parents and siblings, whom we encounter at the very beginning of our life. Very often, we find that when we are in our thirties during a different incarnation, we deliberately choose the people who then accompany us into our next life from childhood on. We choose them as if out of our own forces. In other words, in the middle of our preceding lifetime, we selected those people who have now become our parents and siblings.

This is a very interesting situation. It is remarkable that relationships with people we meet do not remain the same in successive incarnations, nor do we always encounter them at the same age. Nor is exactly the reverse true. In the beginning of one incarnation we encounter, not the people we met at the end of another lifetime, but the ones we met in the middle of it. That is, neither the people we encounter at the beginning of life nor toward the end of it, but rather the people with whom we are coming into contact at midlife, are those who surrounded us as blood relations at the beginning of an earlier incarnation. Those who were together with us at the beginning of that life now appear in the middle of this present lifetime. We can also assume that in the middle of one of our later incarnations, we will meet again with those who stood around us at the beginning of our present life. They will then be related to us as companions freely chosen in some way. Karmic connections are strange indeed!

What I have just said is the result of spiritual-scientific research. But as I have already pointed out, if we use the means indicated by spiritual science to look at the inner connection between the beginning of one incarnation and the middle of another, we can grasp that this is by no means useless or meaningless. Through such things, if we relate to them rationally when they are presented to us, life around us becomes bright and clear. It becomes bright and clear if we are not dull, not to mention "dumb," simply taking everything as it appears. It becomes bright and clear when we somehow try to grasp what meets us in life by making concrete connections. Nevertheless, such connections are not fully understandable as long as we only speak of karma in very abstract and general terms.

It's useful to think about how it happens that in the middle of life we are positively driven by karma to make—with apparent rationality—the acquaintance of some specific person. Doesn't it look as if this happened independently and objectively? This is because this person was a blood relative of ours in an earlier lifetime. Through karma, we are now brought together because we have a connection with each other.

If we weigh each instance in the course of our lives in this way, we will see that this really does allow light to shine into life. Even if we make a mistake once, or even ten times, we can still be right about one particular person we meet in life. And when we realize through such deliberations that we have met this person before in some place or another, this thought becomes like a signpost, pointing the way to other things that also would not have occurred to us otherwise. As more of these things coincide, we become more and more certain of the truth of individual facts.

Karmic relationships cannot be ascertained all at once. Our life's greatest insights, the most important knowledge that illuminates our lives, must be acquired slowly and gradually. Of course, this is something people don't want to believe. It's easier to believe that we could find out suddenly, through some stroke of lightning, that we were together with this or that person in an earlier life, or that I was so-and-so. It may be uncomfortable to think that all this is knowledge that has to be acquired slowly, but that is how it is. Even after we hold the belief that this is how things might be, we must still go on researching. Our belief then acquires certainty. Even when something is already seeming more and more possible in this area, we can still go further by continuing to research. We wall ourselves off from the spiritual world when we succumb to hasty judgments in these areas.

Try to think for yourselves about what was said today concerning acquaintanceships at mid-life, and how they relate to people who were close to us in an earlier incarnation. You will arrive at some very fruitful thoughts, especially if you also consider what is said in my booklet *The Education of the Child.*[1] It will be very apparent that the result of your thinking accords with what is said in this booklet.

A serious admonition must still be added to what has been said today: *True spiritual researchers avoid drawing conclusions.* Instead, they allow things to approach them and test them first with ordinary logic. If this is done, it is impossible for anything to happen similar to what confronted me again recently, something quite characteristic of the way people today would like to approach anthroposophy: A very intelligent man said to me—I say this without irony, and fully recognize that he really is intelligent—"When I read your book, *An Outline of Occult Science,*[2] I must say that it seems so logical, so connected to other facts revealed by the world, that I must frankly say it would also be possible to arrive at these things by simply thinking about them. These things need not be the result of supersensible research. What's said in this book is not questionable; it all corresponds to reality." I was able to assure this gentleman that I did not believe I could have arrived at these facts simply through thinking, and that with all due respect for his intelligence, I did not believe he could have discovered them simply by thinking, either. In fact, although everything in the field of spiritual science can be confirmed by logic, it really is not possible to discover it simply through thinking. There shouldn't be any reason

1. Included in *The Education of the Child and Early Lectures on Education,* Anthroposophic Press, Hudson, NY, 1996.
2. *An Outline of Occult Science.* Anthroposophic Press, Hudson, NY, 1972.

to doubt the spiritual-scientific origin of something just because it is possible to test and grasp it logically! On the contrary, my view is that it should be somehow reassuring that logical thinking can recognize spiritual-scientific communications as undeniably correct. It cannot be the ambition of spiritual researchers to say all kinds of illogical things so that they will be met with belief. You see, spiritual researchers cannot claim to discover these things by means of thinking. But when we think about things that have been discovered by spiritual-scientific means, they can seem very logical. In fact, they seem *too* logical, so we no longer believe that they spring from spiritual-scientific sources. This is indeed the case with anything said to stem from pure spiritual-scientific research.

If what was said here today seems grotesque to you at first, just try to think about these things logically. I really would not have been able to derive all this from ordinary logical thinking if spiritual facts had not led me to it. But once it is there, it can be tested logically. And you will find that the more subtly and conscientiously you test it, the more it will all turn out to be true. Even when accuracy cannot be tested—as is the case with what was said today about parents and siblings from one lifetime and mid-life acquaintances from the next—these things will give the impression of being not only highly probable, but of bordering on certainty, simply through the way different parts relate to each other in the whole. Certainty is especially justified when we test these things in real life. In the case of some people we meet during mid-life, we will see our own behavior and that of the other person in a totally different light, if we meet as if we had been siblings in the previous lifetime. This will make the whole relationship between us much more fruitful than if we merely proceed blindly through life.

Thus we can say that anthroposophy increasingly provides us with more than knowledge and understanding of life, it also supplies indications about how we can take hold of life's circumstances and fill them with light, not just for our own sake but also for the sake of our actions and behavior toward life and our life's task. It's important that we do not believe that this will spoil our spontaneity in life. Only anxious people whose intentions toward life are not fully serious can believe that. We, however, must be clear that by getting to know life more intimately, we can make it richer and more fruitful. Anthroposophy is meant to pull whatever meets us in life into a field of vision that makes all our forces richer, more confident, and more conducive to hope than they were before.[3]

3. Further exercises related to karma can be found in: Joop van Dam, *Coping with Karma,* Hawthorn Press, Stroud, UK, 1991; Athys Floride, *Human Encounters and Karma,* Anthroposophic Press, Hudson, NY, 1983; Rudolf Steiner, *Karmic Relationships: Esoteric Studies*, vol. 2 (lecture May 4, 1924), and vol. 7 (lecture June 14, 1924), Rudolf Steiner Press, London, 1974, 1973.

5

Examples of Karma Working between Two Incarnations

STUTTGART, FEBRUARY 21, 1912

Our questions yesterday touched on human karma, and we attempted to make their connection to processes within the human soul apparent. This is a connection to something attainable, for we saw how it is possible to arrange things experimentally in our soul life, so to speak, and thus call up certain inner experiences that would necessarily lead to a very pronounced conviction that the law of karma is true. It is by no means arbitrary that such questions are repeatedly brought up for us to consider from the anthroposophical point of view. Rather, it is because we will increasingly need to recognize how what we call anthroposophy, in the truest sense of the word, relates to life and human evolution as a whole. For example, if a large number of people acquire the conviction underlying what we considered yesterday, our entire life will gradually have to change, and it is undoubtedly possible to get at least an approximate idea of this change. People who are imbued with such truths approach life differently, and life changes in certain ways as a result. This brings us to the extremely important question—which ought to be a question of conscience for individuals joining the anthroposophical movement—of what makes a person of today an anthroposophist.

Misunderstandings can easily arise when we try to answer this question appropriately, because many people today, including some among ourselves, still confuse the anthroposophical movement with an outer organization of some sort. This is not to say anything against any such outer organization; in a certain way, it must be there in order for anthroposophy to be cultivated on the physical plane. However, it is important to realize the basic possibility for anyone who is serious and honest, who has a deeper interest in the concerns of spiritual life, and who wants to deepen his or her philosophy of life in accord with such a movement, to belong to an outer organization of this kind. Having said this much, it's evident that those who join an organization of this sort must not be required to accept any dogma whatsoever or any specific creed. It is a different matter, however, to point succinctly to what actually makes a modern person, a person of the present day, into an anthroposophist.

Anthroposophical conviction certainly begins with the common conviction that there is such a thing as a spiritual world, and this must always be emphasized wherever we make anthroposophy public, and discuss its tasks, goals, and current mission. But in anthroposophical circles, we must be clear that a person becomes an anthroposophist through something much more specific and definite than the conviction that a spiritual world exists. After all, people have always had this conviction in every circle that was not expressly materialistic. The theosophy of Jakob Boehme and other earlier theosophists, for example, did not yet contain what constitutes anthroposophy for a present-day person. This is something that Western civilization has worked toward with all its might, so that working in this way has become a characteristic feature of many people's striving. On the other hand, however, our outer civilization and people of superficial culture emphatically dispute this very thing which so aptly characterizes the anthroposophist, and regard it as something foolish.

Certainly, we learn a lot through anthroposophy. We learn about the evolution of humanity and about the evolution of our Earth and planetary system. All these things are part of the foundation for someone who is striving anthroposophically. But the struggle to achieve conviction with regard to the issues of reincarnation and karma is what I am referring to as being especially meaningful for the anthroposophist of today. As we move into the future, an essential transformation of our present-day life will come about through the way in which people become convinced of reincarnation and karma and find it possible to make their thoughts of reincarnation and karma carry over into the whole of life. It will create totally new ways of living, totally new ways for people to be together—ways that are necessary if our human civilization is to move onward and upward rather than falling into decline. Inner soul experiences such as those brought to light yesterday are basically something that all modern individuals can attain. If only they have enough energy and strength to do this, they will arrive at an inner conviction of the truth of reincarnation and karma. However, we could say that the actual intentions of true anthroposophy are opposed by the whole superficial character underlying our present times.

This underlying character of our times shows itself most typically, perhaps, in the considerable interest that still exists in the central issues of religion, in the evolution of humanity and the world, and in karma and reincarnation as well. When these issues also extend to the specific individual doctrines of different religious faiths—concerning the nature of the Buddha or the Christ, for example—discussion of them will still be met with widespread interest. But this interest is waning and becoming fundamentally weaker. Even among those who call themselves anthroposophists today, interest greatly decreases when it comes to talking concretely about how anthroposophy is to find its way into all the details of outer life. Basically, this is very understandable. We stand in the midst of outer life, each of us in his or her own position in the world. We could say that the world, as it reveals itself in its current rules and routines, is almost like a single great establishment in which individuals resemble cogs in a machine. That's what they feel like with their work in this world, with their concerns and occupations from morning till night. They know only that they must adapt to the world's outer structure.

Parallel to this, questions appear that must be present for every soul that is capable of looking even slightly beyond what daily life provides—questions about the soul's fate, the beginning and end of its life and its connection to divine spiritual beings, questions about the powers underlying the world. A wide rift, a deep abyss, appears between what our daily life provides—the concerns it causes, and so on—and what we receive in the field of anthroposophy. We might say that for most people, even today's anthroposophists, their anthroposophical conviction hardly coincides at all with what they think and do in daily life. All we need to do is publicly raise some concrete question or other, and deal with it in a spiritual-scientific, anthroposophical way, and we will immediately see that the interest is not present for questions like these—interest that was still present in general religious discussion, and so on. Now, we can't expect anthroposophy to get down to work immediately; we can't expect everyone to be able to put it into action right away. But it must be pointed out that the mission of anthroposophical spiritual science is to introduce and incorporate into life the inevitable results of a soul's gradual conviction that the ideas of reincarnation and karma are realities. In fact, we could designate this as an identifying characteristic of present-day anthroposophists: They are on the way to acquiring a well-founded inner conviction of the active force of the ideas of reincarnation and karma. Everything else, we might say, is a direct result of that.

Of course, we cannot simply think: Now I am going to take what I have gained from reincarnation and karma and tackle outer life with it immediately. That also cannot be. We must, however, acquire concepts of *how* reincarnation and karma necessarily find their way into outer life and become forces that direct it.

Let's take the idea of karma and how it works through a person's different incarnations. Ultimately, we must see the abilities and strengths of people who are coming into the world as the results of causes for which they themselves laid the groundwork in earlier incarnations. If we are consistent with this idea, then we must really treat each individual as a sort of inner riddle: something is swimming in the dark depths of this person's earlier incarnations and has to work its way out. A significant revolution will come about, not only in education but in all aspects of life, when we take such a concept of karma seriously. And if we were to realize this, the idea of karma would be transformed from mere theory into something that truly intervenes in practical life, something that could really become a practical matter.

However, all of outer life as we see it today is an image of human relationships, from which the idea of reincarnation and karma has been excluded. Indeed, ordinary interrelationships actively deny this very idea. Our outer life is organized today in a way that seems intended to suppress any possibility of people arriving at the idea of reincarnation and karma through personal development. For example, there is actually nothing as hostile to a real conviction of reincarnation and karma as the principle of drawing a wage corresponding directly to work performed. This kind of talk sounds strange, very strange, doesn't it? But you must not take this to mean that anthroposophy wants to become radical and immediately throw out the principles of our way of life, and introduce a new order overnight. That cannot be. However, we do need to entertain this thought: In a world order where people believe a direct correspondence between work and recompense is necessary, and that each individual must earn what is needed for life's needs through work, so to speak, a true fundamental conviction of reincarnation and karma can never really flourish. Of course, the status quo must remain for the time being: anthroposophists in particular must recognize that what exists has been called forth in turn by karma, and in this respect it is right and necessary. But they must also be able to comprehend what can and must result from recognizing the idea of reincarnation and karma, germinating like a new seed within the organism of our current world order.

Above all, the idea of karma leads us to feel that we are not inserted into the world order through chance. I believe this proceeds directly from what we considered yesterday. We should not feel it a coincidence to find ourselves in our particular place, but rather that a subconsciously willed decision underlies this, as it were. We should feel that the decision to occupy our present position was made in the spiritual world before we entered this earthly existence, while working our way out of the spiritual world between death and birth. It is a personal prebirth, pre-earthly willed decision that places us in our position in life and inclines us toward the blows of destiny that strike us. When people become convinced of the truth of karmic law, inevitably they begin to feel inclined toward their position in the world, and perhaps even to love it, regardless of what this position may be.

Of course you can say, "This is a strange and remarkable thing to say! This may be true for poets, writers, and others who are culturally active. It's one thing to preach joy, love, and devotion to one's place in life to people like that, but what about all the people who occupy positions in life, positions with content and activities that really do not have a particularly positive effect on people, but instead tend to give these souls the impression that they are among those neglected and subjugated by life?" No one denies that our civilization directs great efforts toward bringing about improvements that are intended to cure our dissatisfaction with our positions in life. How many political movements, and how many religious denominations, are trying to improve life in every way so that outer life on Earth as a whole somehow becomes bearable for humankind?

These efforts, however, all fail to consider one thing: The kind of dissatisfaction necessarily encountered by many people in life today is interrelated in many ways with the whole course of human evolution. Basically, people arrived at a karma such as this because of how they developed in earlier times, and the current state of human cultural development is the necessary result of their different karmas working together. When we try to characterize this state of civilization, we have to say that it is extremely complex. We must also say that what people are doing and the actions they perform have less and less to do with what they love. If we counted the people today who must perform an unloved activity in their outer position in life, we would find their numbers are greater than those who have to admit that they love their outer occupation, that it makes them happy and contented!

Only a short time ago, I heard a man making a remarkable statement to a friend. He was saying, "If I look back over the details of my life, I must say that if I were to start again from childhood and could live life over, exactly as I wanted to, I would do the same thing again. I would do exactly what I have done until now." His friend replied, "Very few people today can say that," which is probably true of most people at present. There are not many of our contemporaries who would pronounce themselves immediately ready to start their life over again with all its joys, sorrows, blows of destiny, and setbacks, and who would be completely satisfied if it offered them exactly the same thing again. We cannot say that this situation—that there are so few people today willing to take up their present karma again in all its details—that this is not related to everything today's civilization has brought to humanity.

Our life has become more complicated, but this has happened through the different karma of individual personalities now living on Earth. There can be no doubt about this. For those with even a little insight into the course of humanity's evolution, there is no reason to expect that we are moving toward a less complicated future life. On the contrary, our life will continue to become more complicated. No matter how much activity is taken from us by machines in the future, our outer life will become more and more complicated; and unless circumstances come about that are very different from those that now affect our culture, very few lives will be happy and content. These different circumstances will have to result from human souls being imbued with the truth of reincarnation and karma.

Through this truth, we will recognize something totally different running parallel to the increasing complexity of outer civilization. What will it take for people to be more and more infused with the truth of reincarnation and karma? What will it take, in such a relatively short time, for the idea of reincarnation and karma to work into our system of education so that even in childhood people adopt this idea, just as they now hold the conviction that the Copernican view of the solar system is correct? This must happen if our civilization is to avoid falling into decline.

What was needed for the Copernican view of the solar system to take hold of human souls? There is something very strange about this Copernican solar system. I don't want to talk about the Copernican view itself, but about how it entered into the world. Just consider the fact that this view of the solar system was developed by a Christian cleric, whose thinking on the subject allowed him to dedicate his work on these ideas to the Pope. It was possible for Copernicus to believe that his thoughts were fully in line with Christianity. Was there any proof of Copernicanism at that time? Could anyone prove what Copernicus had thought? No one could prove it, and yet, think how fast it made inroads into humanity. How long have we been able to prove it, to the extent that it is correct at all? Only since the 1850s, since Foucault's experiment with the pendulum. Before that, there was no proof that Earth rotates. It is nonsense to insist that Copernicus was able to prove everything about the hypothetical insight he formulated, and this also applies to the statement that Earth rotates around its axis.

We were able to conclude that Earth must have been turning under the pendulum, only when we realized that a swinging pendulum tends to persist in its plane of oscillation, despite the Earth's rotation, so that when we allow a long pendulum to swing freely, its direction of oscillation changes in relation to Earth's surface. This experiment, the first real proof that the Earth moves, was performed in the nineteenth century. Before that, it was impossible to see Copernicanism as anything other than a hypothesis. And yet, in spite of the fact that Copernicus believed he could dedicate his work to the Pope, its effect on the nature of the human soul in more recent times caused it to remain on the Index until 1822.[1] The work on which Copernicanism is based was not taken off the

---

1. *Index Expurgatorius* and *Index Librorum Prohibitorum* were lists of books generally forbidden to members of the Catholic Church.

Index until 1822, but this was still before the existence of any real proof of the Copernican view. The force with which the Copernican view of the solar system found its way into human souls compelled the Church to acknowledge it as non-heretical.

It has always seemed profoundly characteristic to me that, as a little boy in school, I first learned of the Earth's movement from a clergyman, not a teacher. And who can doubt that the Copernican view has lodged itself even in the hearts and minds of children, though now is not the time to speak of the truths and errors of this view.

In this same way, the truth of reincarnation and karma must lodge itself in our hearts and minds if civilization is not to fall into a decline. However, humanity has less time for this than it had for the acceptance of Copernicanism. And those who call themselves anthroposophists today are called upon to do their part so that the truth of reincarnation and karma can flow even into the hearts and minds of children. This is not to say that anthroposophists with children are now to teach this as dogma. Insight into these things is required.

There is a reason why I mentioned Copernicanism: we can learn how to make the idea of reincarnation and karma a cultural success from what made Copernicanism successful. What contributed to making Copernicanism spread so quickly? I am now going to say something terribly heretical, something that is an abomination for modern people. The point is, however, that for anthroposophists, anthroposophy must be as serious and significant as Christianity was for the first Christians, who were also in conflict with what existed at the time. If anthroposophy is not taken this seriously by its adherents, it will not be able to do what must be accomplished for humanity's sake.

And so I have to say something horrible: The Copernican view of the solar system that people now learn about was able to lodge in human souls because a superficial person could believe in this system. Superficiality is part of what it takes to be quickly convinced of Copernicanism. This is not to deny the great merit of Copernicanism or its significance as a first class cultural phenomenon. The intent is not to downplay the significance of Copernicus for humanity. Not at all, and yet it can be said that it is not necessary to be a very profound person in order to believe in Copernicanism, because it does not require developing oneself more inwardly, but rather more outwardly. And it truly takes a high degree of superficiality on the part of the human mind to come up with statements as trivial as those found in modern monistic books, which state with a certain enthusiasm that the Earth we human beings inhabit is but a speck of dust in the cosmos compared to other bodies in the universe. This tirade is trivial for the simple reason that this speck of dust with all its details concerns human beings on Earth, while other things spread out in the cosmos and compared to Earth are of little concern to us. Human evolution had to take a totally outward and superficial direction in order to quickly become capable of accepting Copernicanism, so to speak.

But what must we do to make the teachings of reincarnation and karma our own? These teachings must meet with success much more quickly if humanity is to avoid falling into decline. But what will it take for these teachings to find their way into the hearts and minds of children?

Superficiality and turning outward were needed for Copernicanism, and turning inward is needed for us to live our way into the truths of reincarnation and karma. We must be able to receive seriously things such as we discussed yesterday. We must be able to enter into our inner soul experiences, into the intimacies of the mind, into what each soul must experience in the most profound inner depths and core of its individual being. The consequences of Copernicanism for modern culture are on display everywhere today, in all the popular media; it is seen as a particular success that this can also be offered to people in the form of pictures, preferably motion pictures. This in itself characterizes how incredibly superficial this culture has become.

When it comes to intimate aspects of the truths summed up in the words "reincarnation" and "karma," little can be communicated in pictures. People become convinced of reincarnation and karma by turning inward and developing things such as those spoken about yesterday. The opposite of what is current in modern superficial culture is needed for ideas of reincarnation and karma to find their way into humanity. This is why it is so necessary to insist that this turning inward actually takes place in the field of anthroposophy. Although certain schematic representations are undeniably useful for rationally grasping fundamental truths, it must nevertheless be said that the most important thing in the field of anthroposophy is to consider the laws working in the soul's depths. They work in the soul's forces, just as outer physical laws work in the outer world of time and space.

But basically, people today still understand very little about these individual laws of karma. This can be read between the lines of things repeated over and again today in outer culture. What enlightened person in the outer culture would not imagine that humanity has transcended its childhood stage—when it *believed*—and has now entered its mature phase, and is able to *know*? Things like this are repeatedly proclaimed and do a great deal to fool people out there, but anthroposophists should no longer be deluded by expressions such as "Faith must give way to knowledge."

All these tirades about faith and knowledge fail to consider what can be called karmic connections in life. When someone capable of esoteric research looks around at particularly devout and devotional present-day personalities, and asks, "Why is this person especially devout? Why does this person possess a religious fervor and enthusiasm that is tantamount to genius in religious devotion, in directing his or her thoughts to the supersensible world?"—when these questions are posed, the answer is remarkable. In the case of naturally devout people whose faith may have first appeared as an important phenomenon later in life, if you go back to their earlier incarnations, you discover the remarkable fact that they were people of knowledge then. Their previous incarnation's knowledge, its rational element, has been transformed into the element of belief in this current incarnation. This is one of those noteworthy karmic phenomena that seem especially strange when contrasted with another fact. Pardon me if I say something which, though not shocking to any of those sitting here, would certainly shock many outsiders who swear by and are only ready to accept what their senses and brain-bound reason present to them. When we approach especially materialistic people who no longer believe, but want only to *know*—and this is a very mysterious situation—we find apathy and dullness in their previous incarnation. Actual investigation of their different incarnations yields the strange result that, whereas enthusiastic believers—not fanatic, yet steadfastly accommodating their human nature to the higher worlds—build their present faith on the basis of knowledge acquired in previous incarnations, materialistically based knowledge is acquired through being deaf and dumb to any world-view from earlier incarnations.

Just imagine how our whole view on life changes when we lift up our gaze from what we experience in the immediate present to what the human individuality experiences going through different incarnations! Much of what we pride ourselves on in our current incarnation looks strange in connection with how it was acquired in the previous incarnation. When looked at from the standpoint of reincarnation, many things do not appear so unbelievable; we only need to examine how a person evolves within one incarnation under the influence of these inner soul forces. We only need to observe the power of faith, the soul power people can have through believing in something supersensible that transcends ordinary sensory phenomena. No matter how much the idea may be resisted by modern materialistic monists, who say that only knowledge counts, while faith has no basis in certainty—with regard to these people, another fact holds true: Faith as a state of soul has an enlivening effect on our astral body, while lack of faith—inability to believe—causes the astral body to dry up. The effect of faith on the astral body is like that of nourishment on the physical body. Isn't it important to realize what faith can do for a person's health of soul, and also of the body, since a healthy soul affects physical health?

Is it not strange that on the one hand we want to do away with faith and make room for knowledge, while on the other, a person who cannot believe necessarily acquires a hardened, dried-out astral body? It is possible to really take a look at this within the scope of a single lifetime, since we don't need to survey successive incarnations to recognize that a person with no faith acquires a dried-out astral body. It's enough to have an overview of that person in one incarnation. We can thus say that lack of faith dries up our astral body; we impoverish ourselves through lack of faith and deplete our individuality in the next incarnation. Lack of faith makes us unreceptive, and for the duration of the next incarnation, incapable of acquiring knowledge.

It is vain, dry, and empty logic to say that knowledge is in conflict with faith. For those with insight into these things, all the trivial things that have been said about faith and knowledge have about as much significance as a discussion between two people in which one claims that until now, men have been of greater significance for human evolution, while the other says the same about women. Thus, in humanity's infancy, one sex was supposedly more significant, while now it is the other. For those who know the spiritual facts, it is clear that knowledge and faith are related in the same way that the two sexes are related in outer physical life. To see correctly, we must look at this as a clear and significant fact. The parallel goes this far: We have emphasized that, generally alternating between being male and female, an individual changes sexes in successive incarnations. Similarly, a more devout incarnation is also usually followed by a more rational one, then a more devout one again, and so on. There are exceptions, of course, so it is possible to have several male or female incarnations in succession. As a general rule, however, these things are mutually fruitful and complementary.

However, other human forces are similarly complementary. We will describe one such force as the ability to love, while its complement is the inner strength that permits a person to have self-esteem, inner harmony, and the self-confidence to know what he or she has to do in life. Here also, the effect of karma is to alternate incarnations. In one incarnation, it develops an individual's selfless love for his or her surroundings, a kind of self-forgetting or dissolving into the surroundings. This kind of incarnation will alternate with those in which the individual again feels increasingly called upon not to get lost in the outer world, but to grow stronger inwardly and apply that strength to personal progress. Of course this should not degenerate into lovelessness, just as self-forgetting should not degenerate into completely losing oneself. Again, these two things belong together. And it is also absolutely permissible to emphasize again and again that it's not enough for anthroposophists to want to make a sacrifice. Many people are only too ready and willing to make sacrifices, but in order to make a meaningful sacrifice for the world, a person must first have the necessary strength. A person must first *be* something before sacrificing him or herself; otherwise, the sacrifice of oneself is not worth much. In certain ways, this is a kind of egotism, though muted—that is, taking the path of least resistance and not struggling to perfect oneself, not continuing to strive to accomplish something worthwhile.

I ask you not to misunderstand this—it might seem that we are preaching lovelessness. It is very easy for the external world today to accuse anthroposophists of striving to perfect their souls, to make progress with regard to their own souls—in short, of becoming egotists. It must be admitted that many quirks, deficiencies, and mistakes can appear in the course of people's striving for perfection. Very often, what appears among anthroposophists in the name of personal development is not worthy of sympathy. This striving often conceals an extraordinary amount of unacceptable egotism.

It must be emphasized that we live in an age and culture that is lavish to the point of abandon with its willingness to sacrifice. Although lovelessness is present on all sides, there is also an incredible waste of love and self-sacrifice that occurs. This must not be misunderstood; we must be clear that love can be very much misplaced if it doesn't appear together with wise conduct of one's life and wise insight into the circumstances in question. In such cases, it can do more harm than good.

We live in an age when many people again need something to enter their souls, to help their souls progress; they need something of what anthroposophy contributes to enriching the contents of their souls. For the next incarnation as well as for what takes place between death and rebirth, humanity must strive for new deeds that are not derived from the past. These things must be considered with great earnestness and true dignity, for it is incontestable that the mission of anthroposophy is to be a cultural seed that must sprout and grow into the future. We can best see how that takes place in life when we look at karmic relationships such as faith and reason, love and self-esteem. Many people are convinced that when we pass through the gate of death, we immediately become part of an otherworldly eternity existing somewhere outside of this world—a belief quite in compatible with the development of our age. Those who are convinced of this will never be able to fully acknowledge the soul's progress, and will say to themselves, "If there is any progress, you cannot shape it in any comprehensive way, since you are only transient. You are in this world for a short while, and your only task is to prepare yourself for the other world."

Nevertheless, it's true that we become wisest about life from what we have done wrong. We learn from what we have done wrong; we gain the most wisdom precisely from what we have not succeeded at. Ask yourself seriously, "How often do I have the opportunity to repeat what I have done wrong in exactly the same situation as before?" Very seldom. And wouldn't life be utterly senseless if the wisdom we can acquire from our mistakes were lost to earthly humanity? Life only makes sense if we can come back again and apply the life experience acquired in an earlier lifetime to a totally new life. This is why it's senseless to strive for the perfection of the soul—senseless not only for this earthly existence, if it is seen as the only one, but also for the eternity beyond Earth.

Most of all, it is senseless for those who believe all existence ends after we pass through the gate of death. What kind of strength, energy, and certainty in life it would give people to know that they could apply their strength, which seems to be lost, in a new life!

Modern culture is the way it is because very little was accumulated for it in people's earlier incarnations. Souls have become truly impoverished in their successive incarnations. Where does this impoverishment come from?

Let's look back to ancient times, before the Mystery of Golgotha, when ancient clairvoyance and magical will-forces still existed. That was how it was even into the Christian era. But only the evil aspect, the demonic aspect, still loomed out of the higher worlds during the last ages of ancient clairvoyance. Everywhere in the Gospels, we see demonic natures appearing in the surroundings of Christ Jesus. What had been present in human souls in ancient times as their original connection to divine-spiritual forces and beings was now lost to them. Then the Christ entered humanity. People living now have experienced two, three, or four incarnations since that time, depending on their karma. Christianity has had to work as it has until now because of the presence of weak and empty souls in humanity. Christianity could not develop inner power because weak souls were present in human evolution. We can assess how this came about by looking at another wave of human civilization, the wave that led human evolution to Buddhism in the East. Buddhism includes belief in reincarnation and karma, but includes it in such a way that it sees the task of human evolution only as freeing people from life as quickly as possible.[2] In the wave that was active in the East, the urge to exist was no longer present. We can see how everything that made

---

2. Rudolf Steiner's discussion of Buddhism in this lecture reflects the approach to Buddhist philosophy and practice as it had been expressed within intellectual circles in Europe at the time (1912). In particular, Theravada (previously called Hinayana) was the teaching most widely available to Europeans at that time, which teaches that the main objective for Buddhist practice is to escape the *wheel of life*, or continued incarnations, and to attain *nirvana*, understood by most Europeans at that time to mean "extinction" or "oblivion." Mahayana Buddhism, on the other hand, encourages a vow to reject one's own personal escape from the "wheel of life" until all sentient beings attain nirvana, or enlightenment.

people enthusiastic and decisive about their earthly mission had faded away among the members of the wave of civilization that carried Buddhism. And if Buddhism were to become especially widespread in the West, this would indicate the presence of numerous souls who are among the weakest and least fit for life, for those are the souls who would adopt it. The appearance of Buddhism in any form in the West would be a sign that souls were not able to come to grips with their earthly mission and were trying to escape from it as quickly as possible.

While Christianity was spreading in southern Europe, it was also adopted by northern peoples whose souls had strong instinctive power. At first when they took up Christianity, it could only develop its outer aspects—those aspects that make it especially important for people in present-day culture to achieve a deepening of the Christ impulse, so that this impulse becomes the innermost force of the human soul itself. Thus the soul continually becomes richer and more inward as it goes into the future. Human souls had been going through weaker incarnations, and at the beginning, Christianity was an outer support for them. Now a time has come when souls must become inwardly strong and forceful. In the more distant future, it will make relatively little difference what a soul does in outer life. On the other hand, it will be important for each soul to find and deepen itself, to acquire concepts of how the inner aspect carries over into outer life and of how we can permeate our earthly mission with the consciousness and inner strength gained by being imbued with the truths of reincarnation and karma.

Even if ideas of reincarnation and karma can only penetrate our life in a modest way to begin with, these modest beginnings are incredibly important. The more we gain the ability to judge people by their inner abilities, so to speak, and the deeper we can make our life, the more we contribute to the fundamental character of humankind in the future. Outer life is becoming ever more complicated, and this process cannot be arrested, but souls will find their way to each other in their depths. An individual may outwardly carry out some activity that belongs to the soul; this will bring individual souls together in anthroposophical activity and allow them to work toward making anthroposophical life flow more and more into outer culture. We know that all of outer life is strengthened when the soul finds its reality in anthroposophy. That is why people from all walks of life, all different occupations and lifestyles, come together there. The soul of the outer cultural movement itself is created by what meets us in anthroposophy, that is, the ensouling of outer life. An awareness of the importance of karmic law must first enter the soul for this to come about. The more we go toward the future, the more individuals must be able to feel, through this law, the ensouling of all of life.

Because of outer laws and arrangements, leading an outer life becomes so complicated that people no longer know what to do. On the other hand, by being permeated with the law of karma, knowledge will begin to live in the soul so that the soul can make its way through the world from the inside outward. It will be most able to do this where everything is ordered by inner soul life. We know of things in life where everything goes well because each person is following an inner impulse that provides sure guidance. For example, when walking along the street, there is no law that tells individuals to move to the right or the left to avoid bumping into someone else, yet this is not a constant occurrence because there is an inner necessity that people follow when they meet. Otherwise the police would have to stand next to everyone and order them to the right or to the left. Of course in some circles people are trying to mandate that each person always have a police officer on one side and a physician on the other, but it is not yet possible to make this a reality!

We make the best progress when we are following the unrestricted dictates of our inner being, which must be oriented toward respecting other people and keeping their dignity in mind. That can happen only if we understand people with the understanding that is possible when the law of reincarnation and karma is taken into account. Our social life can function on a higher level only when the significance of this law of reincarnation and karma establishes itself in our souls. This is best demonstrated by concrete observation of something like the relationship between devoted faith and knowledge, or between love and self-esteem. It is also demonstrated by an observation such as the one we made yesterday.

It is not without purpose that I wanted to give these lectures yesterday and today. It is not so much a question of what was said; it also could have been said differently. What was said yesterday and today is not of the greatest importance. What does seem important to me, however, is that those who declare their support for the cultural movement of anthroposophy should be so infused with ideas of reincarnation and karma that they acquire awareness of how life will change when an awareness of these ideas is present in every human soul. Our current cultural life has excluded awareness of reincarnation and karma from its development. And the most significant thing that will come about through anthroposophy is that these things will actually take hold of life, permeating our civilization and fundamentally transforming it.

A person of today may say that reincarnation and karma are just a dream, just nonsense—they see how people are born and how they die, but since they don't see anything flying out of people when they die, it doesn't need to be taken into account. Compare someone like this to another who says, "Although we don't see anything flying out, if we consider these laws, we find all of life's processes understandable, and we can explain things that can't be explained otherwise." These two kinds of people are related in the same way that present-day culture relates to the future, which will include the laws and the teachings of reincarnation and karma. As thoughts common to humanity, reincarnation and karma have not played a role in the development of present-day culture; however, these ideas will play a very great role in all future cultures.

Anthroposophists must feel how they are working in this way to help bring forth a new culture; it must be alive in their consciousness. This sensation—this feeling that reincarnation and karma are intensely important for life—can hold a group of people together regardless of their outer circumstances. People who are held together by this attitude can find their way to each other only through anthroposophy.[3]

---

3. The following lecture cycle directly discusses karma as related to anthroposophists and the Anthroposophical Society, as well as to anthroposophy's cultural and spiritual mission within a historical and karmic context on Earth: Rudolf Steiner, *Karmic Relationships: Esoteric Studies,* vol. 3, Rudolf Steiner Press, London, 1977.

6

Vital Questions in the Light of Reincarnation and Karma

BREMEN, NOVEMBER 26, 1910

Today in this branch meeting we will begin with several of life's crucial issues that touch each of us daily. After that, we will rise to higher spiritual viewpoints for a while. I would like to start with two human qualities, two human errors or failings that are experienced as negative, as decreasing a person's worth. We will speak about what we call *envy* and *lying*.

If you look around in life, you will easily notice that as a rule, there is a very natural antipathy to these two human qualities. Also, when we look up to other people as leaders among human beings, we see that they value the absence of these two failings. Goethe, for instance, was very concerned with self-knowledge and thinking about his own mistakes, and mentioned that while he had certain faults and certain assets, what seemed most important to him was that he could not count envy among his failings. And the famous Benvenuto Cellini said that he was glad he didn't need to accuse himself of lying. So we see that these great personalities sensed the importance of struggling against these two human qualities. And even the simplest, most unsophisticated individuals agree with leaders of humanity in their negative assessment of these failings.

If we ask ourselves why these two qualities are so instinctively condemned, we realize that almost nothing else is less compatible with one of the most important earthly qualities; envy and lying are incompatible with what we call *empathy* for other people. When we envy someone, we tend not to yield to the particular virtue devoted to the deepest, inmost kernel of that person's being, to the divine in the other person. Actually, to empathize with someone is of value only when you are also able to appreciate the other person's essence, his or her spiritual being. However, as a basis for empathy, appreciation for others includes recognition of their assets and the ability to take pleasure in their successes and level of development. All of this precludes envy. Envy shows itself to be a quality that is very closely related to an individual's greatest egotism.

Something similar can be said about lying. If we tell an untruth, we break the law that applies to the truth—to create a bond that includes all individuals. What is true is the truth for all human beings. More than anything else, truth allows us to practice the development of a consciousness that includes all human beings. If we tell an untruth, we commit a heinous act against the bond meant to connect one human heart with another.

This is how things look when we consider them from the viewpoint of human beings. When we consider them from the viewpoint of spiritual science, we know that the effects of our earlier incarnations are being worked out in this lifetime, and that we are subject to many different influences. There are two great influences in particular that have to be worked through again and again—specifically, what we call the luciferic and the ahrimanic influences. We will not attempt to cover these from the cosmological point of view today, but will restrict ourselves to the life of human individuals. We will imagine that we have passed through many incarnations and that the power of Lucifer was already working on our astral body when we were going through our very first incarnation. Since then, this luciferic power has always been the power that tempts our astral body. Forces are present that proceed from Lucifer and exert an influence on our astral body. Basically, Lucifer's efforts are directed toward gaining influence over the human astral body on Earth. We can find him in everything that pulls the astral body down, in all the qualities that live in our astral body as egotistical passions, desires, urges, and wishes. Thus, it must be clear that envy is one of Lucifer's worst effects on us. Everything living in our soul that can be counted as envy falls into his territory, and each time we have an attack of envy, Lucifer takes hold of the urges in our astral body.

Ahriman, on the other hand, influences our ether body. Everything to do with disturbances of judgment derives from him—both the unintentional disturbance of arriving at a false judgment, and the deliberate one of lying. When we succumb to lyin,, Ahriman is at work in our ether body.

It is interesting that we feel these influences strongly enough to experience such great antipathy when they appear, and that people will do everything to combat these two qualities of envy and lying. You will not easily find people who consciously admit that they want to be envious. To be sure, "I envy you" has crept into our language as an idiom, but what it means is not so very bad; we do not mean actual envy when we say it. In any case, as soon as we notice envy or lying in ourselves, we do everything we can to combat it, and in doing so we take up the struggle against Lucifer and Ahriman in this particular area.

Often, however, something then happens that we should notice when applying ourselves to spiritual science. We can combat individual attacks of envy and lying, but when these qualities are stuck in our soul—when we have acquired them in earlier incarnations and are now combating them—they then appear as different qualities. When we try to combat a tendency to envy stemming from earlier incarnations, this envy puts on a mask. Lucifer says, "This person has noticed feelings of envy and is fighting me; I'll turn this person over to my brother Ahriman." And then a different influence takes effect, one that is a consequence of combating envy. Qualities that we are struggling against appear in disguise. Often the envy that we are fighting takes the form of an urge to seek out other people's mistakes and to make them aware of them with a great deal of reproach. We encounter many people in our life who always discover the mistakes and negative aspects of others, as if with a certain clairvoyant strength. If we search for the basis of this phenomenon, we find that envy has been transformed into a compulsion to reproach, which the people in question take to be a very desirable quality. It is a good thing, so they say, to make people aware of the presence of their bad qualities. However, there is nothing more behind this compulsion to reproach than transformed envy in disguise. We should learn to recognize whether such qualities are the original ones or whether they are transformations of something else. In the process, we must consider whether such individuals were envious as children—perhaps we drove the envy out of them, and they have now become compulsive reproachers.

Lying also often transforms itself in our lifetime and shows itself in disguise. Lying can make us feel ashamed, but it's not easily uprooted, and very often it metamorphoses into a certain superficiality with regard to the truth. It's important for us to know these things so we can observe what we encounter in another person in life. People like this are satisfied with answers that make us ask, "How can they possibly be satisfied with an answer like that?" It is easy for them to say, "Yes, yes, of course, that's the way it is." Very often, this is the end product of the transformation of a personal tendency toward lying. We need to test the law of karma, particularly with regard to such qualities. People don't pay attention to them, for among all the various beings at work on different planes, human beings are the most forgetful.

For instance, if we are acquainted with a person and remain close over the years, we can observe how some things in this person change. If we are still close after thirty years, we might find noteworthy connections within that person's life when we look back over a lifetime together, while the person in question knows nothing about it, and has forgotten it all. We really should observe such things in life, however. Important connections become evident. For example, a certain person is envious as a child. Later, the envy is no longer evident, but at a later age it appears transformed as a lack of independence in the person in question, of wanting to be dependent on others. It appears in the form of ideas of being unable to stand on one's own two feet, of always needing other people around to advise and help. A specific moral weakness appears as a consequence of the transformation of envy. When someone has this moral weakness, we will always find that this is the karmic consequence of transformed envy.

When transformed, lying creates a shyness later in life. In later life, someone who tended to lie as a child doesn't dare to look people in the eye. Out in the country, people have an instinctive elemental knowledge of this, although it doesn't function on the level of concepts. They say that you shouldn't trust a person who can't look you in the eye. Shyness and reserve that stem not from modesty but from fear of meeting other people are the karmic consequences of lying during the same incarnation.

What appears in this way as a moral weakness within an incarnation has an organizing influence on the next incarnation. The soul's weakness resulting from envy cannot significantly destroy the body during this present incarnation, when the body has already been built up. But when we die and return in a new incarnation, the effect of these forces is such that they become organic weaknesses in building up the new body. We find that people who have possessed transformed envy in a previous incarnation form a weak body. We say without prejudice that a person is weak simply because people need to know what is weak and what is strong. When a person is easily susceptible to different influences and puts up no resistance, then we know that the person's body is weak, and that this weakness is the result of envy that was transformed earlier.

Now we must realize, however, that when a child is born into a particular environment as a weak child, we should not imagine that only this *inner* karma is active, but also that people are brought together in their surroundings for a reason, and not by chance. This aspect of karma—our adaptation to our environment—is extremely easy to see. A flower such as an edelweiss, for example, can only thrive in the environment to which it is adapted, and a human being also thrives only in the environment to which he or she is adapted. The simplest possible logic necessarily tells us this, for we can only understand life when we take this into account. Each being conforms to its environment; nothing is by chance.

Therefore, we are born into the group of people we have envied or reproached; we find ourselves with our weak body among the people we have envied for their accomplishments in a previous incarnation, or something like this. It is infinitely important to know these things, because we understand life only when we include them in our considerations. When a child with a weak body is born into our surroundings, we should ask ourselves how we are meant to relate to this. The right way to relate to it must be the most morally meaningful way—that is, to forgive. This will lead most surely to the goal in this case, and is also the best education for such a person. It has an incredibly educational effect when we can lovingly forgive a weak child who is born into our surroundings. The person through whom forgiveness occurs in a truly forceful way will see that the child becomes stronger and stronger because of it. Loving forgiveness must even affect thinking, because that makes it possible for the child to gather the forces needed to turn old karma around and get it moving in the right direction. Through this the child will also become physically strong. A child such as this often demonstrates unpleasant qualities. The healing effect is strongest when we love the child in the depths of our heart, and we soon find out just how effective the healing is.

Something comparable applies when we look at the other quality: lying. Within a single incarnation, the person who lies becomes shy in later life. This is a soul quality. But in the next incarnation, this quality takes effect as the body's architect. In this case, the child appears not merely weak, but unable to acquire a proper relationship to its surroundings—that is, the child is mentally handicapped. In this case, we must think that we are the people to whom this person often lied, and we must repay the bad that happened to us with the best we can offer. We must try to communicate a great deal of the truths of spiritual life to such a person, and then we see how that person begins to blossom. We must always keep in mind that this individual lied to us a lot in earlier incarnations, and do everything possible to bring about a right relationship between this child and his or her surroundings.

When we consider these things, we find that as human beings we are always called upon to help other people come to terms with their karma in the right way. People understand nothing of karma if they think others must be left to their own karma. If we were to meet individuals who had lied to us, and we were to believe these people must come to grips with their karma by themselves, this would show that we do not have a correct understanding of karma. The right idea would be to provide help wherever possible. When it is said that we should leave people to their karma, this could only apply in the esoteric realm, but never in actual life.

Let's imagine that we would make an effort to help other people according to their individual karma. Take a person with a shy nature. We concern ourselves lovingly with that person, creating a connection between that person and ourselves. We will then see in later life that something comes back to us from this person. We must leave this to karma, however; we are not allowed to hope for it. We must regard it as our obligation to help the other person. At this point we come upon a subtle law: Everything we do to help another person bear and overcome karma not only helps that person, it also does something for us. As a rule, however, what we do for the sake of our own quick progress will not help much. The only thing that can bear fruit for an individual is what he or she does for others. We cannot send good things in our own direction. The best effects come from helping another person overcome his or her karma, since what we do for others is a gain for humanity. We can do nothing for ourselves; that must be done in turn by others. That's why we must understand empathy for other people in the highest sense of the word. If we develop this empathy in the highest sense, then we also feel an obligation to empathize with another person with regard to envy and lying. In this way we develop a feeling of solidarity that extends to all human souls.

In fact, humanity possesses the potential for each human being to always feel a connection to humanity as a whole, and this feeling, in all its different manifestations in life, should also be present and active in the individual's struggles against Lucifer and Ahriman. By helping people whose physical bodies have become weak through the influence of envy that has been overcome, by coming to understand how we should behave toward these people, it can become clear to us that the world is filled with the impulses of Lucifer and Ahriman. How they can be overcome in the course of the Earth's evolution also becomes clear. Anyone who traces such connections in his or her feelings necessarily comes to an ever deepening feeling for all of humanity. The possibility exists, so to speak, for each of us to feel what connects him or her to all human beings. However, this feeling has changed greatly in the course of human evolution.

If we go back three or four thousand years, the feeling of what human beings have in common was very pronounced in everyone. If we go back still further—back through the post-Atlantean cultures, back to old Atlantis, and still further back—we come to an incarnation in which we came down into a physical body for the first time. Before that, we existed in a spiritual state—or so it was still said three or four thousand years ago. At that time, wisdom-filled feelings such as this were to be found in all people. The human soul asked, "What does it mean to be a human being?" And it answered itself, "Before I came down into my body for the first time, I existed in a sea of divine-spiritual interweaving life. I was within it, and all other human souls were within it. That was our common point of origin." This basic feeling in the souls of human beings made it possible for them to feel kinship, to feel that they had something in common with all human beings, because they felt that all human souls had a common origin. And if we recall how all the ancient mystery schools worked on people to make them good people who would be receptive to the most profound, intimate, and moving feelings, we can see that this was always done by pointing to their common origin, to the fact that all human beings proceed from a common divine source. It was easy to sound this note in their souls then, but it became more and more difficult. For example, if this note had been sounded then in the number of people now sitting here, it would have made an overwhelming impression.

But human feeling for our common origin became ever colder. This was necessary because humanity had to pass through a certain point in evolution. And if I describe that point, we will also have to look toward our human future, toward the goal of Earth's evolution.

Just as our origin is common to all of us, just as all human souls sprang from a common source, so too all human souls will come together in a common goal. And how can we reach this goal so that we can continue to evolve once Earth has achieved its own goal and the material sphere beneath us is dissipating and falling away? How can we have a common understanding of this goal so that we proceed into our future together? The awareness of what we have in common will need to extend into the deepest sinews of our soul. This is only possible if we develop a feeling for our future, similar to the feeling people in ancient times had for their human origin, a feeling that is growing ever colder among humanity. Now, the feeling and the certainty of a common goal held by all human beings must come to life more and more in our souls. Regardless of our individual degree of development or where we stand in life, the very fact that we are human beings must make possible a soul experience that allows us to say we are all striving for a single goal. In looking toward this goal, we must also be able to realize that this is something that can concern each and every human being.

In our most profound inner depths, we must be able to find something in which we can all come together in a single point. Esoteric teaching calls this "something" the Christ. People thousands of years ago felt, sensed, and knew that our souls are all born out of a common divine source. Similarly, we will increasingly learn that just as we can be united and come together in something we think in common, something that can live in all human heads, there is also something that can live as a common element in all human hearts, something that can flow through all human hearts like the blood of life. If this pervades us more and more warmly in incarnations to come, these incarnations will then run their course in such a way that Earth, having achieved its goal, will be able to proceed to the next planetary stage—the Jupiter state—and human souls will come together as one in the common element of the Christ.

For this to be a possibility, the Mystery of Golgotha had to take place. In Jesus, the Christ became human so that this common stream of warmth could flow from human heart to human heart. The feeling for our common human goal has its origin in the cross on Golgotha, which connects past and future. This is the goal of future human evolution. It is not important whether we retain the name "Christ" for what we have in common. What is important is that all human beings learn to grasp that the feeling people originally had for their common origin is being transformed into a feeling for our common earthly future.

Earth's evolution is divided into halves—one lasting until the time of the cross on Golgotha, and the other from that time until the end of Earth. We human beings have a great deal to do to grasp the Christ and his evolution. Once these things have been grasped, we as human beings will come together in a common goal for the Jupiter evolution. All the knowledge we have as individuals culminates in finding this principle of the *Christ-like.*

Today we tried to recognize how karma works from one incarnation to another to shape the body. Having done so, we understand how human beings can become more and more perfect as they go through incarnation after incarnation. We are still speaking of the Christ, though without using that name, because we are turning away from the personal element. When we are confronted with a child who lies to us, we ask ourselves how we can help this child transform his or her karma. We do not ask whether being lied to hurts us. We turn to the very center of the child's being, and in doing so we help karma move on. In this way, deep human compassion will increasingly take effect in the world.

Thus, what we call spiritual science—if wealso include in it a real grasp of life's processes related to reincarnation and karma—prepares us to truly grasp the Christ impulse in the world. How people formulate this in words is not important. Those who really understand this evolutionary law cannot help but be Christians, whether they are Hindus or Muslims or belong to some other religious tradition. What's important is that they take this impulse into their souls, the impulse for a common goal for humanity, as in ancient times the impulse to look toward our common human origin was alive in people.

Thus, spiritual science always leads to the Christ impulse. It cannot do otherwise. It would also be possible to summarize spiritual science as it appears today by saying, "Even if those who meet spiritual science want to know nothing of Christianity, in truth they are already being led to the Christ." In reality, that is where they are being led, even if they resist this in words.

Today we have shown our souls something that has a direct connection to life. We have seen how we should act when a child lies or is envious. It must be clear to us that the thread of karma runs through all of the incarnations of a human soul, that its karma is spun according to its destiny. Having looked back to our origin in God, we look to God again when we look ahead to our human goal.

When we look back on the culture of the ancient rishis, we see that they pointed to the human origins, to the world in which human beings existed before descending into incarnation. This teaching persisted for hundreds and thousands of years. The great Buddha taught it when he spoke of how everything that created a connection to the world of our origin has been lost to people because they cling to embodiment. He challenged people to leave the world of embodiment so that their souls could once again live in the spiritual worlds of their origin. The prophets, in announcing the coming of the Christ, also pointed to a future in which human beings would once again discover their proper earthly goal. And then there was the Christ himself, and the act of the Mystery of Golgotha. Through this Mystery of Golgotha, the individual human being can now be led toward our Earth's divine-spiritual future.

Perhaps there is nothing quite as shattering as two similar statements of the Buddha and the Christ, which present to our souls the contrast between the old times and the new. As the Buddha stands among his pupils, he draws their attention to the body and says, "I look back from incarnation to incarnation and see how I have again and again entered a human body such as the one I now wear. Again and again, the temple of this body has been built up for me by the gods. Again and again the soul attempts to enter this bodily temple in new incarnations. Now, however, I know that I no longer need to return to a bodily temple. I know its beams are broken, its pillars collapsed. Through my knowledge, I have freed my soul from this body. The wish and desire to return to such a body has been killed." This was a great and powerful result of the old time of looking back on our human origin. The Buddha, with his pupils and successors, strove to become free of the body. How powerfully different this is from the Christ standing before his intimate pupils and saying, "Tear down the temple of My body, and I will build it up again in three days." These are the words of the Christ, taken at face value, regardless of how we interpret them. The Christ does not long to be free of the temple of the body. He wants to build it up again.

It is not as if the Christ himself would be there again in such a physical body in future incarnations. But what he teaches his pupils and all human beings is to return into this earthly temple again and again in order to make the Christ impulse greater and more intense in each successive incarnation, so that we human beings are able to take up more and more of earthly existence. In the end, we will be able to say that we spent these incarnations working to become more like the Christ. We become more like him by taking into this bodily temple what the Christ permitted to stream forth from his own being from the cross on Golgotha. We allow this to stream from human soul to human soul, for only through this can we understand each other now. This is what all human souls will have in common in our earthly future. And then the time will come when Earth as a planet will cease to exist, will fall into dust, and human beings in a spiritualized state will proceed to their next incarnation on a different planet.

The words of the great Buddha—"I feel how the columns of my bodily temple no longer bear weight, how its beams are breaking apart"—can stand before our souls as the endpoint of our common human origin. And when we turn to what the Christ says to his disciples—"I will build up the temple of this body in three days"—this can be for us like the beginning of the time that points to our earthly goal. We can expand upon this statement, saying: "In death, this temple falls apart, but we know that the best forces we have acquired in this incarnation are used for our next incarnation. We have received these forces by devoting our souls to the knowledge of Christ. In this way, we will always make progress from incarnation to incarnation." When we human beings build up this bodily temple for the last time, we will have arrived at an understanding of our common earthly goal for the future.

It is the Mystery of Golgotha alone that can be the common impulse for humanity as a whole, for human and Earth evolution.

7

The Formation of Karmic Forces

HAMBURG, MAY 26, 1910

To begin with today, I would like to present several rather general viewpoints related to how karma develops. After that we will gradually be able to go more and more into things that can actually only be illustrated through specialized explanations, if I may put it like that. If we want to acquire insight into the course of karma, we must be able to visualize how a person's entire organization is put together during the descent from the spiritual world into the physical world.

I'm sure you understand that there are actually no suitable expressions in modern language for these processes, which are relatively unknown in our modern civilization, and that therefore the words available to express these occurrences are imprecise at best. To begin with, when we descend from the spiritual world into the physical world for a life on Earth, our physical body has been prepared for us by the stream of heredity. Nevertheless, we shall see that this physical body relates in a certain way to what a person experiences between death and a new birth. For today, however, it is enough for us to be aware that this physical body actually comes to us from Earth. In contrast, the parts of the human entity that can be called its higher members—the ether body, astral body and the I—come down from the spiritual world.

A human being draws the ether body together out of the world-ether as a whole, before uniting with the physical body provided by heredity. It's possible for the soul-spiritual individual—that is, the

I, astral body and ether body—to unite with the physical human embryo only because the mother-organism's ether body gradually withdraws from this physical embryo.

So the human being unites with a physical embryo after having drawn together an ether body out of the common world ether. We will be concerned with more exact descriptions of these processes later on. At the moment, however, we are primarily interested in the source of the individual members a human being possesses during an earthly life between birth and death. We have said that our physical organism comes from the stream of heredity and our etheric organism from the world ether out of which it is drawn together. Our astral organism—which remains unconscious or subconscious, so to speak, during a person's earthly life—contains the results of life between death and a new birth.

During life between death and a new birth, in accordance with what we have become during our previous earthly lives, we make contact in a great variety of ways with other human souls, as well as with other spiritual beings of the higher world order who do not descend to Earth in human bodies, but exist in the spiritual world. Everything we bring along from earlier earthly lives corresponds to what we were like and what we did during them, and it elicits sympathy or antipathy from beings we meet as we pass through the world between death and a new birth. It is of great significance for our karma that we not only encounter sympathies and antipathies on the part of higher beings as a result of what we did in previous earthly lives, but above all that we make contact with the human souls with whom we were also in contact on Earth, and that a characteristic mirroring takes place between our being and theirs.

Assume that you had a good relationship with a soul you are now meeting again between death and a new birth. During your earlier earthly lives, everything that goes hand-in-hand with a good relationship was alive in you. Between death and a new birth, this good relationship is then mirrored in the other soul when you meet again. It really does happen that human beings going through life between death and a new birth find themselves mirrored on all sides in the souls with whom they are now living, with whom they also lived on Earth. If you did something good to a person, something is now reflected to you from that person's soul; if you did something bad to that person, something else is reflected. You get the feeling—if I may use the word "feeling" with the reservations I mentioned at the beginning of this discussion—the feeling that you have helped this person's soul along. Your experience of helping, your feelings for this person's soul, the sensations that led to your behavior, your own inner experiences while performing this helpful act—all of these experiences come back to you from that soul. They are reflected to you by this soul. In the case of another soul whom you harmed, what lived in you when you were causing the harm is reflected back.

Your previous earthly lives, especially the last one, are actually reflected for you by the souls with whom you were together, spread out before you as if in a great reflective device. But regarding your life of actions, you have the impression that it is all falling away from you. During the time between death and a new birth you lose, or have actually long since lost, the feeling of I-ness that you had on Earth in a body; you are now getting your feeling of I-ness from all this mirroring that is taking place. You come alive in the reflections of actions in all the souls with whom you were together in earthly life.On Earth, your I was like a point, so to speak. Now, in the time between death and a new birth, it is reflected from the periphery on all sides. You are together with other souls in an intimate way corresponding to the relationships you established with them on Earth.

This is all a reality in the spiritual world. If we walk through a room containing many mirrors, we see ourselves reflected in each one. But we also know that, according to our ordinary way of speaking, these images are not really "there." When we go away, the images do not remain; we are no longer reflected. But what is reflected in human souls does remain. And there comes a time, during the last third of the time between death and a new birth, when we form our astral body out of these reflected images. We draw these images together into our astral body so that when we descend from the spiritual world into the physical, we actually carry in our astral body whatever we have taken into ourselves according to how the deeds from our previous earthly life were mirrored in other souls between death and a new birth. This supplies us with the impulses, however, that push us toward or away from the human souls with whom we are then born again into physical life. This is how the impulse toward our karma in a new earthly life develops between death and a new birth. (Later, when the I is discussed, this process will be considered in greater detail.)

It's possible to trace how an impetus from one life works over into another. Let's take the impulse of love, for example. We can act toward other people out of what we call love. It makes a difference whether we perform deeds out of a mere feeling of duty—out of convention, common decency, and so forth—or act out of a greater or lesser degree of love.

Assume that we manage, during an earthly life, to perform actions that are carried by love, warmed through by love. This persists as a force in our souls. What we then take with us as the result of our actions is mirrored in other souls, and it comes back to us as reflected images, from which we then shape the astral body with which we come down to Earth. In this way, love that streamed out from us during a previous earthly life is transformed into joy that comes back to us from other people. Thus, if we do something to our fellow human beings in one earthly life, something carried by love, so that love streams out of us and accompanies our deeds that help other people, then as we go through life between death and a new birth, what was love flowing outward in one earthly life is transformed in such a way that it becomes joy streaming toward us.

My friends, if you experience joy through another person during earthly life, you can be sure that this joy is the result of love you developed toward that person in a previous earthly life; this joy is now flowing back into your soul during this lifetime. You know how joy warms you inwardly, you know how important joy is in our lives, especially the joy that comes from other people—it warms our life, carries our life, gives our life wings, so to speak. It's the karmic result, the effect of love given out.

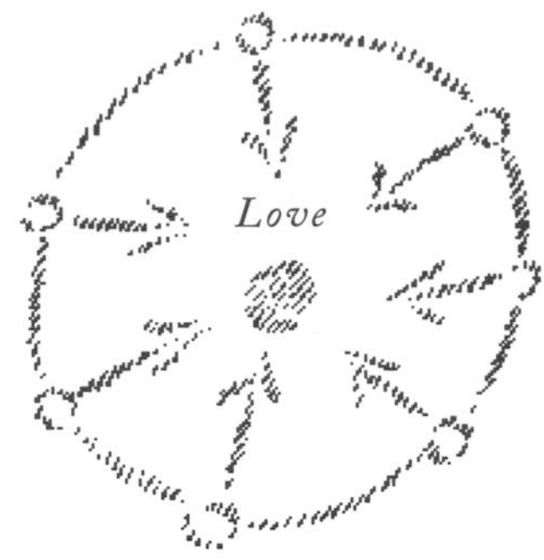

In experiencing this joy, however, we once again connect with the person who is giving us pleasure. In our previous life, we had something within us that made love flow outward; in our present life, the result is an inner experience of the warming quality of joy. This too is something that flows out of us. The impact of a person who is permitted to experience pleasure in life is also something warming for other people. Someone with reason to go through life joylessly is experienced differently than someone allowed to go through life joyfully.

Our experience of joy between birth and death, however, is also mirrored in the various souls we have been together with on Earth, and are then present in our life between death and a new birth. Once again, the reflected image of love works back on us in manifold ways from the souls of people we know. Once again, we carry it in our astral body when we descend into our next earthly life—now the third life in this sequence. Once again, it is engaged in our astral body, imprinted on our astral body. This time, its result becomes the impetus to easily understanding human beings and the world. It becomes the basis of a soul attitude that supports us in our understanding of the world. If we are capable of taking delight and interest in the behavior of other human beings during a particular earthly incarnation—of understanding and finding interest in their behavior—this points to joy during our preceding earthly incarnation, and it points to love in the incarnation before that. People who can go through the world with a free and open mind, allowing the world to stream into them in such a way that they have an understanding of it—such people have acquired this relationship to the world through love and joy.

What we do out of love is something totally different than what we do out of a dry and rigid feeling of obligation. You know how I have always made the point in my writings that truly ethical, truly moral actions, are the ones done out of love.

I have often pointed out the great contrast existing between Kant and Schiller in this respect. In life and in knowledge, Kant actually put hard edges on everything.[1] Through Kant, the entire process of knowing has become full of edges and corners, and the same applies to human actions: "Duty, you great and lofty name, you encompass nothing beloved that ingratiation brings. . . " and so forth. I quoted this passage in my *Philosophy of Freedom*, to the great dissembled annoyance of many of my opponents—not to their real annoyance, just to their dissembled annoyance—and contrasted it with what I was obliged to recognize as my own view: "Love, you impulse that speaks warmly to the soul. . ." and so on.

In contrast to Kant's dry, rigid concept of duty, Schiller wrote, "Gladly I serve my friends, but unfortunately I do it out of inclination, and so it often rankles that I am not virtuous." As we know, according to Kantian ethics there is no virtue in what we do out of inclination, but only in what we do out of a rigid concept of duty.

Now, there are people who are initially unable to love; these people, because they are unable to tell others the truth out of love—when we love other people, we tell them the truth and not a lie—tell them the truth out of a feeling of duty, instead. And because they cannot love, they use their feeling of duty to avoid hitting other people, beating them up or slapping their face when someone does something they don't like. There is a difference between acting out of a rigid concept of duty—though it may often be necessary in our life in society—and acting out of love.

---

1. This is a play on words: the German word *Kante* means "edge." —TRANS.

Actions performed out of a rigid concept of duty or convention, because "it's the right thing to do," don't call forth joy in the next earthly life. Instead, having undergone mirroring by human souls as I described, in the next lifetime they call forth something we might call "a feeling that people are more or less indifferent to you." Many people have to carry this through life, have to suffer from this feeling that they are a matter of indifference to others. And they are right to suffer from other's indifference to them, because human beings are there for each other—we each depend on not being a matter of indifference to others. Their suffering results from a lack of love in a previous lifetime, where they acted like decent human beings because a rigid sense of duty hung over them like the sword of Damocles—I'll call it a wooden sword and not a steel one, because that would be unsettling for most dutiful people.

Now, however, we are at our second earthly life in the sequence. As we have seen, in our third life this second lifetime's joy, which results from love, becomes a free and open heart that brings the world home to us, giving us a free and insightful sense for all that is beautiful, true, and good. But in this third incarnation, what streamed toward us as indifference from other human beings, and what we experienced as a result of this, causes us to not really know what to do with ourselves. When people like this are in school, they do not really know what to make of what the teachers are doing with them. When they are a bit older, they do not know whether they should become locksmiths or cabinet-members. They do not know what to do with their life, so they go through it without any real direction. They are not totally dull with regard to how they perceive the outer world—they can understand music, for example, but do not take pleasure in it. In the end, it doesn't matter to them whether music is more or less good or bad. They can sense the beauty of a painting or some other work of art, but questions such as "What's it good for, anyway?" always nag at their souls. These are things that take place in the third earthly life of this karmic sequence.

Let's assume, however, that a person harms a fellow human being in some way, either out of hatred or out of a tendency toward antipathy. We can imagine all the intermediate stages. Let's say that a person harms a fellow human being out of criminal feelings of hatred; or—leaving out the intermediate stages—he or she could also be a critic. In order to be a critic, you always have to hate a little, unless you are one of those critics who praise people—and they are few enough nowadays because it's not interesting to acknowledge the good in something. Things only get interesting when you make jokes about them. Now, there are all kinds of possible stages in between, but we are concerned here only with human actions that proceed from cold-blooded antipathy. We are often unaware of this antipathy, and it can go as far as hatred. Everything people do in this way to others—or even to subhuman creatures—is given vent in soul conditions, which are also then mirrored during life between death and a new birth. And what comes from this hatred in our next earthly life streams toward us from the world as a distressed nature, as a lack of pleasure that is caused from outside, as the opposite of joy.

You may well say, "But we experience so much suffering! Is that really all supposed to come from a greater or lesser degree of hatred in my last earthly life? I cannot possibly imagine that I was such a bad person that I now experience this much sorrow because I hated so much!" This is what people tend to say. But if you want your thinking on this subject to be unprejudiced, you must make it clear to yourself just how great our illusions are about the extent of our antipathy towards other people. These illusions make us feel good, so we readily give in to them when it comes to imagining away our feelings of antipathy. People are actually going through the world with much more hatred, or at least with much more antipathy, than they think they are. Also, hatred isn't usually experienced initially at all, because it gives the soul some satisfaction, and satisfaction covers up the hatred. When hatred comes back as suffering flowing toward us from outside, the suffering is what we notice.

But just try to imagine, my friends, all the possibilities for hatred that exist, on a quite trivial level, in a gab-fest where half a dozen—that's enough!—aunts or uncles—uncles can gossip, too—when they are sitting around venting their spleen on their fellow human beings. Just imagine how many antipathies are vented on people in the course of an hour and a half, though sometimes it goes on longer. While this is all pouring out, people don't notice it, but they certainly *do* notice it when it comes back in their next earthly life. And inevitably, it does come back.

So a part of what we experience in an earthly life as suffering inflicted from outside—not all of it, since there are other karmic connections we will get to know, but a part of it—can actually stem from our feelings of antipathy in previous earthly lives.

In all this, of course, we must be aware that karma, or any karmic stream, must have a beginning somewhere. For example, if you have a succession of earthly lives:

a b c (d) e f g h

with "d" being the current one, this doesn't mean, of course, that all the pain coming to us from outside originates in a previous earthly life. It can also be an original, initial pain that will only unfold karmically in the next earthly life. That is why I say that a great part of the suffering that flows toward us from outside is the result of hatred we bore in previous earthly lives.

If we move on to the third earthly life, the result of what flows toward us as suffering—but only the result of suffering that comes to us from stored-up hatred, so to speak—the result that is then laid down in the soul is at first a sort of dullness of spirit, a dulling of our insight with regard to the world. When a person encounters the world indifferently and phlegmatically, and doesn't meet things or people with an open mind, it is often the case that the person has acquired this dullness through the suffering caused by his or her own karma in a previous earthly life. This karma in turn resulted—if it is expressed like this in a dull soul-makeup—from feelings of hatred going at least as far back as the earthly lifetime before that. We can always be sure that being stupid in one earthly life is the consequence of hatred in a particular previous earthly life.

But you see, my friends, our understanding of karma should not only be based on our use of it to understand life. We should also be able to use it as an impulse for life, knowing that there is not only an "a, b, c, d" to life, but also an "e, f, g, h." We know that there are earthly lives to come and that the soul contents we develop in our current earthly life will have effects and consequences in our next earthly life. If someone wants to be especially stupid in the lifetime after next, all he or she has to do is to hate a lot in this lifetime. If, however, that person wants to have a free and open mind in the lifetime after next, all he or she has to do is love a lot in this earthly life. Insight into karma, knowledge of karma, only acquires value when it flows into our intentions toward the future, when it plays a future-oriented role in our will.

It is absolutely true that the time has now come in human evolution when the unconscious can no longer go on working the way it did while our souls were going through earlier lives on earth. The age we now live in requires that people become increasingly free and conscious, and in fact, this has been happening since the first third of the fifteenth century. And so for human beings today, the next earthly life will already contain a dim feeling for previous earthly lives. Just as modern people who notice that they are not especially intelligent blame this on heredity rather than on themselves—seeking the cause in their physical nature according to the views of modern materialism—so too the people who will be the reincarnations of those alive at present will have at least the dim, unsettling feeling that if they are not especially intelligent, there must be something present that was formerly connected to feelings of hatred and antipathy.

When we speak of Waldorf education today, of course we must take the present state of earthly civilization into account. We are not yet free to educate people publicly with consciousness of repeated earthly lives as a goal, for people today do not as yet have even a dim feeling for repeated earthly lives. But if the beginnings that are now being made in Waldorf education are taken up and developed further during centuries to come, people will then take into account in ethical and moral instruction that a less-than-gifted child is coming from earlier earthly lives in which he or she did a lot of hating, and they will then use spiritual-scientific means to search for those this child may have hated—since the people who were hated, who had actions directed against them out of hatred, must be somewhere in the surroundings. In the centuries to come, we will have to gradually integrate the process of education much more into human life. We will have to be able to see just where the metamorphosis of lack of understanding, now being lived out, is being mirrored in a child, or has been mirrored during life between death and a new birth. We will then be able to do something at an early age so that a special love develops toward those people who experienced a particular hatred coming from that person in previous earthly lives. We will then see that this person's understanding, and even his or her entire soul constitution, will be illuminated through this concrete application of love.

Looking concretely into a lifetime to note the karmic connections can be helpful in education, and will not lie in general theories of karma. Then we will notice that it isn't a matter of indifference that children are brought together by destiny in a class. And when we get beyond the terrible lack of concern that is the rule today with such things—when we get beyond seeing a class as thrown together, as having landed there by chance rather than as having been brought together by destiny—when we get beyond this terrible lack of concern, then we as educators in particular will be able take into consideration the remarkable karmic threads spun between individuals by their earlier lives. We will then be able to insert into the children's development something that will act as a balance. In a certain respect, karma is something that is subject to an unavoidable necessity. An unavoidable necessity allows us to set up the sequences:

Love—Joy—Open Heart and Mind.
Antipathy or Hatred—Suffering—Stupidity.

These are unavoidable connections. However, it is also true that, just as we confront an unavoidable necessity in the flow of rivers and have nonetheless been able to regulate their flow or give them a different course to follow, so too it is also possible to regulate or influence the flow of karma. That is also possible.

Then when you notice a potential for dullness in a child, it will occur to you to guide the child to develop love in his or her heart. As would already be possible today for people with a subtle gift for observing life, you will discover the other children to whom this child is karmically related and will lead the child to love them in particular and to perform loving actions toward them. You will find that you can equip the child with love as a counterbalance to antipathy, and that in the next incarnation, the next earthly life, this will mitigate the child's diminished mental capacity.

There actually are instinctive educators, so to speak, who often instinctively do something to make poorly endowed children able to love, and thus gradually educate them to be more receptive human beings. Things like this actually transform our insight into karmic connections so that it serves life.

Now, before we go on to consider details of karma, there is another question that must be placed before our souls. Who is the person we know to be karmically connected to ourselves, at least in a general way? I must use a term for this that is often used somewhat mockingly these days: Such a person is our *contemporary*. He or she is on Earth with us at the same time.

When you think about this, you will realize that if you were together with certain people in one lifetime, then you were also together with them in the previous lifetime and also in the lifetime before that; as a general rule anyway—these things can also get shifted around a bit.

On the other hand, the people who will be alive fifty years from now were also together with specific people in their previous earthly lives. According to this line of thinking, the people in sequence B will never come together with the people in sequence A. This is an oppressive thought, but a true one.

People can raise doubts on this subject by pointing to the increasing number of human beings on Earth, and so on. I will address this later. What I want to do now, however, is suggest this thought to you. It may be an oppressive thought, but it is a true one. It is actually so that the ongoing life of human beings on Earth proceeds in rhythms. As a general rule, one wave of people continues from one earthly life into another; another wave of people also continues from one earthly live to another, and the two waves are separated in a certain way. They don't meet each other in earthly life. They do meet in the long life between death and a new birth, of course, but in life on Earth the fact is, we always come down to Earth again in a limited circle of people. Being contemporaries has an inner significance, an inner importance, for reincarnation in particular.

And why is that? I can tell you that this question, which can be grappled with rationally to begin with, really caused me the greatest imaginable pain on a spiritual-scientific level, because of the need to get to the truth of the matter, to the actual inner situation. You can ask yourself—excuse me for using an example that really played a role for me, as it were, in investigating this issue—why you were not a contemporary of Goethe. Not having been Goethe's contemporary, you can generally conclude, according to the truth of the matter, that you have never lived on Earth at the same time as Goethe. He belongs to a different wave of people.

What actually underlies this? Here we have to turn the question around. But in order to turn such a question around, you must have a free and open mind for human interaction in life. You must be able to ask yourself a question, about which I will have a lot to say here in the near future: For an earthly life, how is it to be someone's contemporary; and how is it to only know about someone from history? What is this like?

Now you see that you need a free and open mind to answer this intimate question. What is it like when a contemporary speaks to you or carries out actions that affect you? What about all the accompanying phenomena in your soul? And then, after having acquired the necessary understanding, you need to be able to compare this to what it would be like if you met a personality who is not your contemporary, and perhaps has never been your contemporary in any earthly life. This is not to say that you cannot hold this person in the highest regard, higher than any of your contemporaries. But how would it be if you were to meet this person as a contemporary? How would it be—please excuse the personal example—if I had been a contemporary of Goethe? If you are indifferent to these things and do not understand what it means to be someone's contemporary, you cannot very well answer this question, but if you are not totally indifferent to them, you can ask how it would be if you were walking down Schiller Lane in Weimar in 1826 or 1827, let's say, and the "fat privy councillor" came walking toward you. Now you know quite well you wouldn't have been able to stand it! You can *stand* your contemporaries, but you cannot stand someone who is not a contemporary; in a certain respect, it would be like poison for your soul life. You can only tolerate him because you aren't his contemporary, but someone who comes before or after him. To be sure, when you have no feeling for these things, they remain in the subconscious. You can imagine that if you had a fine sense for spiritual things, you would know that if you had gone walking down Schiller Street in Weimar and had met fat Privy Councillor Goethe with his double chin, had met him as if he were a contemporary, you would have had a kind of impossible feeling inside. Someone with no sensitivity for this, however, might simply have said "Hello."

So you see, these things do not come from earthly life, because the reasons why it's not possible for us to be the contemporaries of some individual do not lie within earthly life. You have to be able to look into the spiritual connections, and that's why they sometimes seem paradoxical from the perspective of earthly life. But that's how things are. That is absolutely the way things are.

I can assure you that I wrote a preface on Jean Paul with loving devotion, a preface that was published in Cotta's *Library of World*

Literature. But if I had ever had to sit with Jean Paul himself in Bayreuth, I would have most certainly had stomach cramps. This doesn't prevent me from holding him in the highest regard. This is true for everyone, but remains subconscious for most people—remains in the astral or ether body, and doesn't take hold of the physical body. A soul experience that needs to take hold of the physical body must also come to consciousness. But you must be aware, my friends, that if you want to acquire knowledge about the spiritual world, you will not be able to avoid hearing things that seem grotesque or paradoxical, simply because the spiritual world is different from the physical world.

Of course it's easy to make fun of my claim that I would have had stomach cramps if I'd been Jean Paul's contemporary and had sat together with him. Of course, for the ordinary, banal, materialistic world of earthly life, this is the natural response, the absolutely correct response. However, the laws of the banal, materialist world do not apply to spiritual connections. You must become accustomed to using other forms of thought if you want to understand the spiritual world. You must become accustomed to experiencing absolutely surprising things. When our ordinary consciousness reads about Goethe, it's natural that we feel compelled to say, "Oh, how I would like to have known him personally, to have shaken his hand," and so on. This is thoughtless, for there are laws that predestine us to a certain age on Earth, the ability to live in this particular age. Just as we are predestined to live in the specific atmospheric pressure required by our physical body, and cannot go above Earth into an atmospheric pressure not suited to us, so it is also impossible for a person predestined for the twentieth century to live in Goethe's time.

This is what I wanted to say about karma to begin with.

8

Reincarnation of the Spirit and Destiny

from *Theosophy*, CHAPTER TWO[1]

The soul lives and acts in the middle ground between body and spirit. The impressions reaching the soul through the body are fleeting, only present as long as the body's organs are open to things of the outside world. My eyes perceive the color of a rose only as long as they are open and face-to-face with the rose. The presence of both the external object and the bodily organ is necessary for an impression, a sensation or a perception to come about.

However, what I recognize in my spirit as true about the rose does not pass away with the present moment. This truth is not at all dependent on me—it would be true even if I had never experienced that rose. Whatever I may recognize through the spirit is grounded in an element of the soul's life, connecting the soul to a universal content, a content that reveals itself within the soul, but is independent of its transitory bodily basis. Whether this content is imperishable in every respect does not matter; what matters is that it can be revealed in such a way that the soul's independent imperishable aspect is involved, rather than its perishable bodily basis. The soul's enduring aspect comes into view when we become aware of experiences that are not limited by its transitory aspect. Here, too, the important point is not whether these experiences first come to consciousness through transitory bodily processes,

1. Anthroposophic Press, Hudson, NY, 1994.

but whether they contain something that, although it lives in the soul, still possesses a truth independent of any transitory perceptual processes.

The soul stands between the present and the permanent in that it occupies the middle ground between body and spirit. However, it also mediates between the present and the permanent. It preserves the present for remembrance, wresting it away from perishability and giving it a place in the permanence of its own spiritual nature. The soul also puts the stamp of permanence on the temporal and temporary, since it does not simply give itself up to fleeting stimuli, but also determines things out of its own initiative, and incorporates its own essence into its activities. Through memory, the soul preserves yesterday; through action, it prepares tomorrow.

If my soul were not able to hold the red of the rose through memory, it would have to perceive this red over and over again to be conscious of it. But whatever remains after the external impression is gone, whatever my soul can retain, can once again become a mental image or representation, independent of the external impression. Through this ability, my soul turns the outer world into its own inner world by retaining the outer world through memory, continuing to lead an inner life with it, and independent of any impressions acquired in the past. Thus the life of the soul becomes a lasting consequence of the transitory impressions made by the outer world.

But actions also acquire permanence once they have been stamped on the outer world. When I cut a branch from a tree, something that happens because of my soul totally changes the course of events in the outer world. Something quite different would have happened to that branch had I not intervened by my action. I have called up a series of consequences that would not have been present without me, and what I have done today will remain in effect tomorrow. It has become lasting through my action, just as yesterday's impressions have become lasting for my soul through memory.

In our ordinary consciousness, we do not usually form the concept, "becoming persistent through action" in the same way that we form a concept of memory as "becoming persistent through observation or perception." But isn't that I just as strongly linked to a change in the world resulting from its own action, as it is to a memory resulting from an impression? The I assesses new impressions differently according to whether or not it has memories of one thing or another. However, as the I, it also enters into another relationship with the world that depends on whether it has carried out one particular action or another. Whether or not I made an impression on someone through something my action depends on the presence or absence of something in the relationship between the world and my I. In my relationship to the world I am a different person once I have made an impression on my environment. We do not notice this as easily as we notice how the I changes through acquiring a memory, only because as soon as a memory is formed it unites with the whole soul life we always regarded as our own; the external consequence of an action, released from this soul life, continues to work through aftereffects quite different from what we remember about the action. In spite of this, we must admit that something is now in the world as a result of our completed action, its character stamped on it by the I.

Thinking this through carefully, we arrive at a question: Could it be that the results of our actions, whose character has been impressed on them by the I, have a tendency to come back to the I in the same way an impression preserved in memory comes to life again when an outer circumstance evokes it? What is preserved in memory is waiting for a reason to reappear. Could it be the same with things in the outer world that persist because of the character of the I? Are they waiting to approach the soul from outside, just as a memory waits for a reason to approach from within? This is only posed here as a question, since these results, laden with the character of our I, may well never have any reason or opportunity to meet our soul again. However, if we follow this line of thought carefully, we can immediately see that such results could exist, and by their very existence determine the world's relationship to the I. The next thing to investigate is whether anything in human life suggests that this conceptual possibility points to an actual reality.

• • •

Looking first at memory, we can ask how it comes about. Obviously, the process is quite different from how sensation or perception comes about. Without eyes, I could not have the sensation of blue. However, my eyes do not give me any memory of blue; for them to provide the sensation, something blue must be in view at this moment. My bodily nature would allow all impressions to sink back into oblivion if something were not also taking place in the relationship between the outer world and my soul: the forming of a current mental image through the act of perception, with the result that, through inner processes, later I may again have a mental image of whatever originally brought about the mental image from *outside*. People who are practiced at observing the soul will realize it is all wrong to say, "If I have a mental image today, the same mental image will show up again tomorrow in my memory, having stayed somewhere inside me in the meantime. On the contrary, the mental image that I have right now is a phenomenon that passes away with the present moment. But if memory intervenes, a process takes place in me, resulting from something additional that has taken place in the relationship between me and the outer world, something other than the evoking of the current mental image. The old mental image has not been "stored" anywhere; the one my memory calls up is new. Remembering means being able to visualize something anew; it does not mean that a mental image can come to life again. What appears today is something different from the original mental image. I make this point because in the field of spiritual science it is necessary to form more precise concepts about certain things than we do in ordinary life, or even in ordinary science. Remembering means experiencing something no longer there, linking a past experience to present life. This happens in every instance of remembering. Suppose I recognize someone I meet because I met him or her yesterday. This person would be a total stranger to me if I could not link the image formed through yesterday's perception to my impression of today. Today's image is given to me by perception, that is, by my sensory system. But who conjures yesterday's image into my soul? It is the same being in me who was present at both yesterday's encounter and today's. Throughout the preceding discussion, this being has been called *the soul.* Without this trusty keeper of the past, every external impression would be a new one for us. The soul imprints on the body the process by which something becomes a memory. The soul must first imprint, however, and then perceive its imprint just as it perceives something outside itself. In this way, the soul is the keeper of memory.

As the keeper of the past, the soul is continually collecting treasures for the spirit. I can distinguish right from wrong, because being human, I am a thinking being capable of grasping truth in my spirit. The truth is eternal; even if I were continually losing sight of the past and each impression were new to me, the truth could still always reveal itself to me again in things. But the spirit in me is not restricted to the impressions of the moment; my soul widens the spirit's field of vision to include the past. And the more my soul can add the past to the spirit, the richer the spirit becomes. The soul passes to the spirit what it has received from the body. Thus, at every moment of its life, the human spirit carries two very different elements: the eternal laws of the true and the good and the recollection of past experiences. Whatever the spirit does is accomplished under the influence of these two factors. Therefore, if we want to understand a human spirit, we must know two different things about it—first, how much of the eternal has been revealed to it, and second, how many treasures from the past it holds.

These treasures do not remain in an unchanged form for the spirit, however. The impressions we gain from experience gradually fade from memory, but their fruits do not. For example, we do not remember all the experiences we went through as children learning to read and write, but we would not be able to read or write now if we had not had these experiences and if their fruits had not been preserved in the form of abilities. This is how the spirit transforms its treasure trove of memories. It abandons to fate anything that only leads to images of individual experiences, keeping only the force to enhance its own abilities. We can be sure that not a single experience goes to waste, since the soul preserves each one as a memory, and the spirit extracts from each one whatever it can use to enhance its abilities and enrich its life. The human spirit grows as these experiences are worked over and assimilated. Thus, although we do not find our past experiences preserved in the spirit as if in a treasure vault, we do find their effects in the abilities we have acquired.

• • •

Until now, we have been considering the spirit and soul only between birth and death, but we cannot leave it at that. That would be like considering the human body only within these same confines. Of course much can be discovered within these limits, but we will never be able to explain the human form through what exists between birth and death. This framework cannot build itself up directly out of mere physical substances and forces; it must descend from another form—or *Gestalt*—that, like itself, has come about through reproduction. Physical substances and forces build up the body during its lifetime, while the forces of reproduction enable it to bring forth another body of the same form—that is, one that can be the carrier of the same life body. Every life body is a repetition of its immediate ancestor: because this is so, the form the life body assumes is never arbitrary, but is the one it has inherited. The forces that have made my human form possible came from my ancestors.

But the human spirit also assumes a definite *Gestalt* (the words are of course being used here in a spiritual sense). Human spiritual forms are as different as they can possibly be; no two individuals have the same spiritual form. Our observation in this realm must be as calm and objective as it is on the physical plane. We cannot maintain that the spiritual differences in people result only from differences in their environment, their upbringing, and so on. That is not true at all, because two people from similar environments and of similar educational backgrounds can still develop in very different ways. We are forced to admit that they must have begun life with very different endowments.

At this point we are confronted with an important situation that, if we recognize its full implications, sheds light on the essential nature and constitution of the human being. Of course if we choose to turn our attention only to the material aspect of events, we could say that individual differences in human personalities result from genetic differences in the reproductive cells they develop from. If we consider the laws of heredity discovered by Gregor Mendel and developed further by others, this viewpoint can indeed seem very plausible, as well as scientifically justifiable. However, such a viewpoint only demonstrates a lack of insight into how we really relate to our experience. Careful observation of the pertinent details will show that outer circumstances affect different people differently through something that never directly interacts with their material development. A precise researcher in this field will see that what proceeds from material potentials is separate and distinct from what may originate in our interaction with our experiences; this takes shape only because the soul itself enters into the interaction. Clearly, the soul relates to something in the outer world that, through its very nature, has no connection to genetic potentials.

In our physical *Gestalt*, we are different from animals, our fellow creatures on Earth. Within certain limits, however, all human beings have a similar form; there is only one human genus and species. No matter how great the differences between races, tribes, peoples, and personalities may be, physically the similarity between two human beings is always greater than that between a human being and an animal of any species. Everything that comes to expression in the human species is determined by heredity, passed down from one generation to the next. Our human form is bound to this heredity. Just as a lion can inherit its physical form only from its lion ancestors, we can inherit ours only from our human ancestors.

The physical similarity between human beings is apparent to the eye, and the difference between human spiritual forms is equally apparent to the unbiased spiritual view. This is demonstrated by the very obvious fact that human beings have biographies. If we were nothing more than members of our species, no individual biographies would be possible. A lion or a pigeon is of interest only as a member of the lion or pigeon species; we understand everything essential about the individual once we describe the species. It does not really matter whether we are dealing with a parent, child, or grandchild—what is interesting about them is common to all three generations. Human individuality is significant and only begins, however, when he or she stops being merely a member of a genus and species and becomes an individual. I certainly cannot grasp the essential nature of Mr. John Doe by describing his son or his father—I have to know his own personal biography. If we think about the nature of biography, we will realize that spiritually, each human being is his or her own individual genus.

Of course, if "biography" is interpreted as nothing more than a superficial listing of events and experiences, we might well insist that it would be possible to write the biography of a dog in the same sense as that of a person. However, if a biographer captures a person's uniqueness, it will be clear that this biography of one human being corresponds to the description of an entire animal species. Obviously something resembling a biography can be written about an animal, especially an intelligent one, but that is not the point. The point is that a human biography corresponds to the description of an animal species rather than to the biography of an individual animal. Some people will always try to refute statements like this by saying that people who work with animals—zookeepers, for instance—are well aware of individual differences between animals of the same species. Such comments, however, demonstrate only an inability to distinguish individual differences from differences that can be acquired *only* through individuality.

Just as genus and species, in a physical sense, can be understood only when we've grasped that they are determined by heredity, the individual spiritual being can be understood only in terms of a similar *spiritual heredity*. I possess my physical human form because I am descended from human ancestors. But where does that which is expressed in my biography come from? As a physical human being, I repeat the form of my ancestors, but what do I repeat as a spiritual human being? If we insist that my biography encompasses what must simply be accepted as it is, and that it needs no further explanation, we might as well also claim to have seen a hill out there where lumps of matter stuck themselves together into a living human being.

As a physical human being, I descended from other physical human beings; I have the same form as the rest of the human genus. This shows that the characteristics of a genus are acquired within it through heredity. But as a spiritual human being, I have my own particular form, just as I have a personal biography. Therefore, I cannot have acquired this form from anyone other than myself. And since I came into this world, not with general, but with very specific predispositions of soul that determined the course of my life as revealed by my biography, my work on myself cannot have begun at birth. I must have been present as a spiritual individual before my birth. I was certainly not present in my ancestors, because as spiritual individuals they are different from me, and their biographies cannot explain mine. Instead, I, as a spiritual being, must be the repetition of an individuality whose biography can explain mine.

The only other conceivable possibility would be that I had only a spiritual life before birth (or conception) to thank for molding what my biography holds. However, this idea would only be justifiable if we assume that what works on a human soul from its physical environment has the same character as what the soul receives from a purely spiritual world. This assumption contradicts precise observation, however. A human soul receives influences that work on it from physical surroundings, in the same way that earlier experiences in our physical life receive influences from similar new experience. To observe these relationships correctly, we must learn to perceive that some impressions in human life work on the soul's potentials in the same way that, standing before a new task affects what we have already repeatedly practiced in physical life. Rather than affecting abilities acquired through practice in the course of this life, these impressions affect *potential* abilities of the soul. If we achieve insight into these things, we arrive at the idea that earthly lives must have preceded this one. In thinking about it, we can no longer be content to assume that this life is preceded only by purely spiritual experiences.

Schiller carried a physical form that he inherited from his ancestors; this physical form could not possibly have grown up out of the Earth. The same is true of Schiller as a spiritual individuality; he must have been the repetition of another spiritual being whose biography accounts for his, just as human reproduction accounts for his physical form. The human physical form is a repetition or reembodiment, over and over again, of what is inherent in the human genus and species. Similarly, a spiritual individual must be a reembodiment or reincarnation of one and the same spiritual being, for as a spiritual being, each person is his or her own species.

We can object that what has been said here is a mere arrangement of thoughts, and we can demand external proof, as is the custom in ordinary science. However, it must be pointed out that the reincarnation of the spiritual human being is a process that does not belong to the domain of outer physical facts but takes place exclusively in the spiritual domain, and of all our ordinary mental powers, only thinking has access to this realm. If we refuse to trust the power of thinking, we will never be able to explain higher spiritual facts to ourselves. But for anyone whose spiritual eye is open, the above train of thought is just as compelling as any process taking place in front of our physical eyes. Those who find so-called "proof," as construed by ordinary scientific knowledge, more persuasive than what has been presented about the significance of biography may well be great scientists in the usual sense of the word, but they are far removed from the methods of true spiritual research.

The attempt to explain a person's spiritual attributes as an inheritance from parents or other ancestors is evidence of a very dubious prejudice indeed. Those who are guilty of assuming that Goethe, for instance, inherited anything essential to his nature from his father and mother will probably not respond to reason, since they harbor a deep antipathy toward unbiased observation. Their materialistic persuasion prevents them from seeing relationships between phenomena in the correct light.

What has been presented so far provides the prerequisites for tracing our essential being beyond birth and death. Within the confines of life between birth and death, the human being belongs to the three worlds of bodily nature, soul nature, and spirit nature. The soul forms the link between body and spirit by permeating the body's third member, the soul body, with the capacity for sensation, and as the *consciousness soul*, permeates the first spiritual member, the *spirit self*. Throughout life, therefore, the soul participates in both body and spirit, and this participation is expressed in all aspects of its existence. The organization of the soul body determines to what extent the sentient soul can unfold its capacities; on the other hand, the consciousness soul's own life determines the extent to which the spirit self can develop within it. The better the soul body's development, the better the sentient soul can develop its interaction with the outer world; the more the consciousness soul supplies the spirit self with nourishment, the richer and more powerful the spirit self becomes. During life, the spirit self is supplied with this nourishment through experiences, worked-over and assimilated, and through their fruits, as was demonstrated. Naturally, this interaction between soul and spirit can only take place where the two intermingle—that is, in the joining of the spirit self and the consciousness soul.

Let us look first at the interaction between the soul body and the sentient soul. As we have seen, although the soul body is the most finely fashioned aspect of our bodily nature, it still belongs to, and is dependent on this bodily nature. In one respect, the physical body, the ether body, and the soul body form a totality. Therefore, the soul body is also subject to the laws of physical heredity through which the body receives its form; but since it is the most ephemeral aspect of our physical nature, it must also show the most ephemeral manifestations of heredity. Human physical bodies differ only slightly on the basis of race, nation, and family, and although individual ether bodies vary more, they still show a great similarity. However, when it comes to the soul body, the differences are already very great. We perceive a person's external personal uniqueness expressed in the soul body. Therefore, the soul body is also the carrier of whatever personal uniqueness is passed down from ancestors to descendants.

It is true that the soul, as described, leads a full and independent life of its own—it encloses itself with its likes and dislikes, emotions and passions. It is active as a totality, however, and the sentient soul also bears the stamp of this totality. Thus, because the sentient soul permeates and fills the soul body, so to speak, the soul body takes shape according to the nature of the soul and is then able to transmit, through heredity, the predecessor's inclinations, passions and, so on, to the descendants. Goethe's saying: "From my father, I get my build and the tendency to take life seriously; from my mother, my happy disposition and delight in storytelling,"[2] is based on this fact. But his genius, of course, did not come from either of his parents. This gives us an idea of what kinds of soul qualities are, in effect, turned over to the line of physical heredity.

The substances and forces of the physical body are present in the very same way all around us in external physical nature—we are continually taking them in from outside and returning them again. Over the course of a few years, all the substances that make up the physical body are renewed. They are continually renewed, yet they always take the form of a human body, because the ether body holds them together. And the ether body's form is not determined solely by processes taking place between birth (or conception) and death, but is also dependent on the laws of heredity extending beyond birth and death. Because the soul body can be influenced

---

2. "*Vom Vater hab ich die Statur, des Lebens ernstes Führen; vom Mütterchen die Frohnatur, die Lust zu fabulieren.*"

by the sentient soul, characteristic soul qualities can also be transmitted through the line of heredity—that is, the soul has an impact on the process of physical heredity.

And what about the interaction between soul and spirit? During life, the spirit is bound to the soul in the way described earlier. From the spirit, the soul receives the gift of living in the True and the Good, enabling it to bring the spirit itself to expression in its own life—in its inclinations, drives, and passions. The spirit self brings the eternal laws of the True and the Good to the I from the world of the spirit. By means of our consciousness soul, these laws are linked to the soul's own individual life experiences. These experiences are transitory, but their fruits are lasting; the fact that they have been linked to the spirit self makes a lasting impression on it. If the human spirit then approaches an experience and finds it similar to another it has already been linked to in the past, it recognizes something familiar in it and knows it must behave differently toward this than if it were for the first time. This is the basis of all learning. The fruits of learning are the abilities we acquire; this is how the fruits of our transitory life are imprinted on our immortal spirit.

Are we somehow aware of these fruits? Where do those potentials—described above as characteristic of the spiritual human being—come from? Surely they can only be based on the various capacities people bring with them when they set out on their earthly journey. In some ways, these capacities are quite like the ones we can acquire during our lifetime. Take the case of a genius, for instance: As a boy Mozart could write from memory a long piece of music he had heard only once. He was able to do so only because he could survey the whole thing all at once, as a totality. In the course of our lifetime, we can all—at least within certain limits—broaden our capacity to gain an overview of things and understand the relationships between them. We then possess new abilities. Lessing, for example, said that through his gift for critical observation, he had acquired something very close to genius. If we are not inclined to see such abilities, rooted in inborn potential, as miracles, we must see them as the fruits of what the spirit self has experienced through a soul. They have been impressed on the spirit self, and since it didn't happen in this lifetime, it must have happened in a previous one.

Each human spirit is a species in its own right. Just as individual human beings pass on their characteristics, the spirit passes on its characteristics within its species—that is, within itself. *In each life the human spirit appears as a repetition of itself, with the fruits of its experiences in earlier lifetimes.* Thus this lifetime is the repetition of others, and brings with it what the spirit self has gained in its previous life. When the spirit self takes in something that can develop into fruit, it imbues itself with the life spirit. Just as the life body reproduces the form of a species from generation to generation, the life spirit reproduces the soul from one personal existence to the next.

So far, the discussion has shown the validity of the idea that certain processes in human life can be explained in terms of repeated Earth lives. The full significance of this idea can be realized only through the kind of observation that stems from spiritual insights, such as those acquired by following the path to knowledge described at the end of this book.[3] It should be pointed out that ordinary observation, properly guided by thinking, can lead us to this idea, although at the beginning the idea will remain shadowlike, and will not be able to completely defend itself against objections that arise from imprecise observation by improperly guided thinking. On the other hand, anyone who comes to this idea through ordinary thoughtful observation is preparing for supersensible observation by beginning to develop something necessary for supersensible observation, just as we must have eyes before physical observation is possible. And people who object that we talk ourselves into believing in the reality of supersensible perception by conceiving an idea like this only prove themselves incapable of really taking up the truth through independent thinking; they are talking themselves into believing their own objections.

• • •

---

3. Chapter Four, "The Path to Knowledge" in Rudolf Steiner's *Theosophy*.

This is the way the soul's experiences become lasting, not only within the confines of birth and death but also beyond death. But the soul imprints these experiences not only on the spirit lighting up within it, but also on the outer world through its actions, as has been pointed out. What someone did yesterday is still present today in the form of its effects.

Along these lines, the metaphor of sleep and death gives us a picture of the connection between cause and effect. Sleep has often been called "the younger brother of death." I get up in the morning. The continuity of my activity has been interrupted by the night. Under normal circumstances, I cannot resume my activity arbitrarily—I must link up with what I did yesterday if my life is to have any order and cohesiveness. Yesterday's actions are now the conditions I must abide by in what I do today; through what I did yesterday, I have created my destiny for today. I have disengaged myself from my own activity for a while, but it belongs to me and pulls me back again after I have withdrawn from it for a while. My past continues to be connected to me; it lives on in my present and will follow me into my future. Instead of waking up this morning, I would have to be created anew, out of nothing, if the effects of my actions from yesterday were not meant to be my destiny today. It would be as absurd as if under ordinary circumstances I had had a house built for myself and then did not move into it.

But we are not created anew each morning, nor is the human spirit created anew as it starts the journey of its earthly life. We must try to understand what really happens when we set out on this journey. A physical body appears, having received its form through the laws of heredity. This body becomes the vehicle for a spirit that is repeating an earlier life in a new form. Between spirit and body, leading a self-contained life of its own, stands the soul. It is served by its likes and dislikes, its wishes and desires, and places thinking in its service. As the sentient soul, it receives impressions from the outer world and carries them to the spirit, which extracts and preserves their fruits. The soul plays a mediator's role, in a sense, and its task is accomplished in playing this role satisfactorily. The body forms impressions for the soul, which reshapes them into sensations, stores them in the memory as mental images, and passes them on to the spirit to be made lasting. The soul is what actually makes us belong to this earthly life. Through the body, we belong to the physical human genus; we are members of this genus. With our spirit, we live in a higher world. The soul binds the two worlds together for a while.

On entering the physical world, the human spirit finds itself, not in an unfamiliar setting, but in one that bears the imprint of its actions. Something in this new setting belongs to the spirit—bears the stamp of its being, is related to it. Just as the soul once conveyed the outer world's impressions to the spirit to be made enduring, it also, as the spirit's organ, transformed its spirit-given faculties into actions that, in their effects, are equally enduring. In doing so, the soul actually flowed into these actions. The human soul lives on in the effects of its actions in a second, independent life. This gives us grounds for examining how the processes of destiny enter into life. Something happens to us, "bumps into us," enters our life as if by chance—or so we tend to think at first. However, we can become aware that each of us is the result of many such "chance" occurrences. If at the age of forty I take a good look at myself and refuse to be content with an empty, abstract concept of the I while pondering my soul's essential nature, I may well conclude that I am no more or less than what I have become through my experiences until now, as a matter of destiny. I probably would have been a different person if, at age twenty, I'd had a different series of experiences than what actually did happen to me. I will then look for my I, not only in its developmental influences that come from within, but also in what exerts a formative influence on my life from outside. I will recognize my own I in what "happens to" me.

If we impartially give ourselves to such a realization, only one more step is necessary in our intimate observation of life, before we can see something taking hold of the I from outside—coming to us through certain destiny experiences—just as memory works from inside to allow past experiences to light up again. In this way, we gain the ability to recognize a destiny experience as a past action of the soul finding its way to the I, just as a memory is a past experience reinvoked by outer circumstances, finding its way into our minds as a mental image.

The idea that the results of the soul's actions may meet the soul again has already been discussed as a possibility on page 120. However, a meeting of this sort is excluded from the limits of a single life on Earth, because that life has been organized and prepared specifically to bring about the *action*. The experience is intertwined with the *accomplishment* of the action. It is as impossible for a specific consequence of this action to return to the soul as it is for us to remember an experience when we are still in the midst of it. Rather, in this connection, our experience of *consequences* meet the I when it does not have the same gifts it had during that lifetime in which the action was performed—that is, it is only possible to focus on consequences that come from other earthly lives. As soon as we sense that some apparently chance experience is as closely related to the I as anything that takes shape out of the inner being of the I, we can only conclude that in such an experience of destiny, we are confronting consequences that come from earlier lives on Earth. As we can see, an intimate, thought-guided approach to life leads us to adopt the idea (paradoxical as it may seem to our ordinary consciousness) that what we experience as destiny in one lifetime is related to our actions in previous earthly lives. Once again, the full import of this idea can be realized only through supersensible knowledge, without which it remains shadowy at best. But here too, an idea acquired through ordinary consciousness prepares our soul to witness its full truth through genuine supersensible perception.

However, only one part of my action is out in the world; the other part is in me. We can take a simple parallel from the field of biology to clarify the relationship between an I and its actions. Certain caves in Kentucky are inhabited by animals that were able to see when they first ventured in, but have lost their sight through prolonged living in darkness. Their eyes have stopped functioning;

the physical and chemical activity that occurs with sight no longer takes place in them, and the stream of nutrients that once supported this activity has been redirected to other organs. Now these animals can live only in caves. Through their original action—migrating into the caves—they determined the conditions under which they must now live. Their migration has become a part of their destiny or fate. A being that was active in the past has linked itself to the results of its own actions. It is the same with the human spirit. Only by being active could the soul transmit certain capabilities to the spirit; these capacities correspond directly to actions. An action carried out by the soul gives it the strength and potential to carry out another action, which is the direct fruit of the first. The soul carries this around as an inner necessity until the second action has been completed. We could also say that through an action, the need to carry out its consequence is impressed on the soul.

Through its actions, each human spirit has truly prepared its own destiny. It finds itself linked in each new lifetime to what it did in the previous one. We may wonder how that is possible, since the reincarnating spirit finds itself in a world totally different from the one left behind. However, when we ask such a question, the way we conceive of the chain of destiny clings to quite external and superficial aspects of life. If my field of activity is shifted from Europe to America, I will also find myself in totally new surroundings, and yet my life in America will still be quite dependent on how I used to live in Europe. If I was a mechanic in Europe, my life in America will take shape quite differently than it would if I was a banker. In the first example, I will probably be surrounded by machinery again in America; in the second, by the trappings of the banking business. In each case, my former life determines my surroundings; it extracts from the entire surrounding world those things related to it, so to speak. It is the same for the spirit self. In a new life, it is obliged to surround itself with things it is related to from its previous life.

That is why sleep is a helpful image for death, because during sleep we are also withdrawn from the arena in which our destiny awaits us. While we sleep, events in this arena continue without us, and for a while we have no influence on the course they take. Nevertheless, how we live the next day still depends on the effects of what we did the day before. In reality, our personalities are reembodied anew each morning in the world of our actions. It is as if, during the night, we were separated from what is spread out around us during the day. The same holds true for our actions in earlier incarnations. They are bound to us as our destiny, just as dwelling in dark caves has bound the animals to the loss of their sense of sight through migrating into those caves. Just as these animals only can live in the surroundings in which they now find themselves, surroundings they have inserted themselves into, a human spirit can only live in the environment it has created for itself through its own actions. The ongoing course of events sees to it that when I wake in the morning, I find myself in the situation I created the previous day. Similarly, my reincarnating spirit's relationship to surrounding objects, insures that I enter an environment corresponding to my actions in the previous life.

From the above, we can form an idea of how the soul is incorporated into the overall human organization. The physical body is subject to the laws of heredity. The human spirit, on the other hand, must reincarnate over and over again, and its law consists in having to carry the fruits of previous lifetimes over into following ones. Our souls live in the present, although this present life is not independent of our previous lives, since each incarnating spirit brings its destiny along with it from previous incarnations, and this destiny determines the present life. The impressions our souls will be able to receive, which of our desires can be fulfilled, what joys and sorrows will be our lot, whom we will meet—this all depends on what our actions were like in earlier incarnations of the spirit. People to whom our souls were connected in one lifetime will necessarily encounter us again in a later one, because the actions that took place between us must have their consequences. Souls once associated will venture into reincarnation at the same time. Thus, the soul life is a product of the spirit's self-created destiny.

The course of a human life between birth and death is determined in three different ways, and we are likewise dependent on three factors beyond birth and death. The body is subject to the laws of *heredity*; the soul is subject to self-created *destiny* or, to use an ancient term, to its *karma*; and the spirit is subject to the laws of *reincarnation* or repeated Earth lives. The interrelationship of body, soul, and spirit can also be expressed as follows: The spirit is immortal; birth and death govern our bodily existence in accordance with the laws of the physical world; and the life of the soul, which is subject to destiny, mediates between body and spirit during the course of an earthly life. These three worlds to which we belong will be the subject of the next section of this book[4], since some familiarity with them is a prerequisite for all further knowledge of the essential nature of the human being.

If we grasp life's phenomena through our way of thinking, and do not hesitate to follow thoughts resulting from living—vital observation through to their final ramifications—we can indeed arrive at the idea of repeated earthly lives and the law of destiny through mere logic. It is true that for a seer with opened spiritual eyes, past lives are present as direct experience, as if reading from an open book; but it is equally true that the truth of all of this can come to light for anyone with an active, observant reasoning ability.

ADDENDUM

The statements in this chapter on reincarnation and karma attempt to convey the extent to which human life and destiny, in and of themselves, point to the idea of repeated Earth lives. The intent was to do so by thoughtfully considering the course of human life without referring to the spiritual-scientific ideas presented in other chapters. Of course the very idea of reincarnation and karma will seem rather questionable to anyone who only considers ideas well founded, if they assume the existence of only a single Earth life.

---

4. Chapter Three, "The Three Worlds," in *Theosophy*.

However, the intention of this chapter is to show that such ideas cannot lead to an understanding of why a person's life takes a particular course. Thus we are forced to look for different ideas, that may appear to contradict our usual ones. The only reason to avoid looking for them would be our fundamental refusal to apply the same thoughtful consideration with which we investigate physical processes to processes that can only be grasped inwardly. This refusal would mean, for instance, that we belittle the fact that how we experience a stroke of destiny resembles our experience of memory meeting an event that we actually recollect. But if we try to see how a stroke of destiny is really experienced, we can distinguish between the reality and what can be said about such an experience from a merely external viewpoint, denying any vital connection between this stroke of destiny and our I. Viewed externally, a stroke of destiny appears to either be chance, or determined from outside. And since some destiny events are actually making their first impact on a human life, so to speak, and will only show results later on, the temptation is all the greater to generalize from such instances without taking any other possibility into account.

We begin to consider other possibilities only after life has educated our cognitive abilities and brought them into line with what Goethe's friend Knebel once wrote in a letter:

> On close observation, we find that most people's lives contain a plan that seems laid out for them, either in their own character or in the circumstances that guide them. No matter how changeable and varied their situations may be, in the end a certain wholeness or inner coherence is apparent.... The hand of a specific fate, no matter how its working is hidden, it may still be clearly seen, whether moved by outer causes or by inner impulses. In fact, often we are moved in its direction for quite conflicting reasons. No matter how confused the course of a life may be, a plan and a direction still show through.[5]

---

5. K. A. Varnhagen von Ense & T. Mundt, eds., *K.L.von Knebels Literarischer Nachlass und Briefwechsel*, 2nd ed., 1840, vol. 3, p. 452.

Raising objections to this kind of observation is easy, especially for people unwilling to consider the inner experiences from which it stems. However, the author of this book believes that in what he has said about destiny and repeated Earth lives, he has accurately delineated the boundaries within which it is possible to form conceptions about the causes shaping human life. He has pointed out that the conviction to which these thoughts lead is only sketchily defined by them, and that all they can do is prepare our thinking for what must ultimately be discovered through spiritual research. As long as this thought preparation does not exaggerate its own importance or attempt to prove anything, but only trains our souls, such preparation will restrict itself to an inner effort that is unbiased, and can make us receptive to facts we would otherwise simply consider foolish.

Bibliography

Works by Rudolf Steiner:

Anthroposophy (A Fragment), Anthroposophic Press, Hudson, NY, 1996.

An Autobiography, Steinerbooks, Blauvelt, NY, 1977.

Christianity As Mystical Fact, Anthroposophic Press, Hudson, NY, 1997.

How to Know Higher Worlds: A Modern Path of Initiation, Anthroposophic Press, Hudson, NY, 1994.

Intuitive Thinking as a Spiritual Path: A Philosophy of Freedom, Anthroposophic Press, Hudson, NY, 1995.

An Outline of Occult Science, Anthroposophic Press, Hudson, NY, 1972.

A Road to Self-Knowledge and The Threshold of the Spiritual World, Rudolf Steiner Press, London, 1975.

Theosophy: An Introduction to the Spiritual Processes in Human Life and in the Cosmos, Anthroposophic Press, Hudson, NY, 1994.

The Archangel Michael, Anthroposophic Press, Hudson, NY, 1995.

The Child's Changing Consciousness As the Basis of Pedagogical Practice, Anthroposophic Press, Hudson, NY, 1996.

Cosmic Memory: Prehistory of Earth and Man, Steinerbooks, Blauvelt, NY, 1987.

The Education of the Child and Early Lectures on Education, Anthroposophic Press, Hudson, NY, 1996.

The Four Mystery Plays, Rudolf Steiner Press, London, 1982.

From Jesus to Christ, Rudolf Steiner Press, London, 1991.

Geographic Medicine and The Double: Two Lectures, Mercury Press, Spring Valley, NY, 1979.

The Gospel of St. John, Anthroposophic Press, Hudson, NY, 1962.

The Gospel of St. John and It's Relation to the Other Gospels, Anthroposophic Press, Spring Valley, NY, 1982.

Guidance in Esoteric Training, Rudolf Steiner Press, London, 1994.

Health and Illness, Volume 2, Anthroposophic Press, Hudson, NY, 1983.

The Karma of Materialism, Anthroposophic Press, Hudson, NY, 1985.

The Karma of Vocation, Anthroposophic Press, Hudson, NY, 1988.

Karmic Relationships: Esoteric Studies, vols. 1–8, Rudolf Steiner Press, London, 1972–1974.

Life between Death and Rebirth, Anthroposophic Press, Hudson, NY, 1968.

Manifestations of Karma, Rudolf Steiner Press, London, 1969

Nutrition and Health, Anthroposophic Press, Hudson, NY, 1987.

Practical Advice to Teachers, Rudolf Steiner Press, London, 1988.

Reincarnation and Karma: Two Fundamental Truths of Human Existence, Anthroposophic Press, Hudson, NY, 1992.

The Souls' Awakening, Ruth and Hans Pusch, trans., Anthroposophic Press, Hudson, NY, 1995.

Truth and Knowledge: Introduction to "Philosophy of Spiritual Activity," Steinerbooks, Bauvelt, NY, 1981.

Verses and Meditations. Rudolf Steiner Press, London, 1993.

WORKS BY OTHER AUTHORS:

Allen, Paul and Joan deRis Allen, *The Time is At Hand!*, Anthroposophic Press, Hudson, NY, 1995.

Bryant, William, *The Veiled Pulse of Time*, Lindisfarne Press, Hudson, NY, 1996.

Evans, Dr. Michael and Iain Rodger, *Anthroposophical Medicine: Healing*, Thorsons, London, 1992.

Emerson, Ralph Waldo, *The Complete Writings of Ralph Waldo Emerson*, Wise, New York, 1929.

Emmichoven, F. W. Zeylmans van, *The Reality in Which We Live*, René Querido, trans., New Knowledge Books, Sussex, 1964.

McDermott, Robert A., *The Essential Steiner,* HarperSanFrancisco, 1984.

Floride, Athys, *Human Encounters and Karma,* Anthroposophic Press, Hudson, NY, 1983.

Gardner, John Fentress, *American Heralds of the Spirit: Emerson, Whitman, and Melville*, Lindisfarne Press, Hudson, NY, 1992.

Lehrs, Ernst, *Man or Matter: Introduction to a Spiritual Understanding of Nature on the Basis of Goethe's Method of Training, Observation, and Thought*, Rudolf Steiner Press, London, 1985.

Lievegoed, Bernard, *Phases: The Spiritual Rhythms of Adult Life*, Rudolf Steiner Press, London, 1993.

Moody, Raymond, *Life after Life*, Mockingbird, Atlanta, 1975.

Novalis, *Hymns to the Night / Spiritual Songs*, George MacDonald, trans., Temple Lodge Press, London, 1992.

Ritchie, George, *Return from Tomorrow,* Fleming Revell, Old Tappan, NJ, 1978.

Roszell, Calvert, *The Near-Death Experience*, Anthroposophic Press, Hudson, NY, 1992.

Thoreau, Henry David, *The Correspondence of Henry David Thoreau,* Bode and White, ed., Greenwood Press, Westport, CT, 1974.

———*Walden and Other Writings*, Bantam, NY, 1983.

Traherne, Thomas, *Centuries*, Harper & Brothers, New York, 1960.

Van Dam, Joop, *Coping with Karma*, Hawthorn Press, Stroud, UK, 1991.

Welburn, Andrew, *The Beginnings of Christianity,* Floris Books, Edinburgh, 1991.

———*Gnosis: The Mysteries and Christianity*, Floris Books, Edinburgh, 1994.

Index

Rudolf Steiner

(1861–1925)

During the last two decades of the nineteenth century the Austrian-born Rudolf Steiner became a respected and well-published scientific, literary, and philosophical scholar, particularly known for his work on Goethe's scientific writings. After the turn of the century he began to develop his earlier philosophical principles into an approach to methodical research of psychological and spiritual phenomena. His multifaceted genius has led to innovative and holistic approaches in medicine, science, education (Waldorf schools), special education, philosophy, religion, economics, agriculture (Biodynamic method), architecture, drama, new arts of eurythmy and speech, and other fields. In 1924 he founded the General Anthroposophical Society, which today has branches throughout the world.

. . . .

RENÉ QUERIDO, former director of Rudolf Steiner College, a major center in Fair Oaks, California for the study of anthroposophy and the preparation of Waldorf teachers, brings to the editing of this volume more than four decades of spiritual-scientific practice, including particularly the esoteric study of biography. One of the purposes of this volume is to help the reader to take up the challenge of spiritual research concerning the evolution of the individual human soul and spirit throughout evolving spiritual-cultural contexts. Such a study can prove tremendously revealing as well as spiritually necessary for meaning in a time of increasing intellectual confusion and spiritual poverty.

ROBERT MCDERMOTT, president of the California Institute of Integral Studies since 1990, has been professor of comparative philosophy and religion since 1964. His published writings include *Radhakrishnan* (1970), *The Essential Aurobindo* (1974) and *The Essential Steiner* (1984), the "Introduction" to William James, *Essays in Psychical Research* (1986), and "Rudolf Steiner and Anthroposophy" in Antoine Faivre and Jacob Needleman, eds., *Modern Esoteric Spirituality* (1992). He was president of the Rudolf Steiner Institute (1983-94), served as chair of the board of Sunbridge College (1986-1992) and Rudolf Steiner College (1990-1996), and currently serves on the Council of the Anthroposophical Society in America.

About the Cover

The illustration on the front cover is based upon the seventh of seven "seal-pictures," which were displayed for the first time at the 1907 Munich Congress of the Theosophical Society. Originally painted by Clara Rettich from sketches given to her by Rudolf Steiner, these seals, according to Steiner, are not arbitrary symbols. They represent actual facts of the astral world, depicting the astral archetypes of human evolution on earth. Of the present seal Steiner wrote:

> Seal VII is a reproduction of the "Mystery of the Holy Grail." It is that astral experience which renders the universal meaning of human evolution. The cube represents the world of space, yet not mingled with any physical being or event. In the eyes of spiritual science, space is not merely a void, but the vehicle in which the germs of everything physical are invisibly hidden. Out of it the whole physical world is, as it were, precipitated, as salt is deposited from a transparent solution. And, as regards the human being, that which is developed out of space passed through evolution from what is low to what is higher. Out of the three space-dimensions, expressed in the cube, grow first of all the lower human powers, illustrated by the two serpents; these again bring forth out of themselves the purified higher spiritual nature, represented in the world spirals. The upward growth of these higher powers makes it possible for a human being to become the recipient, or chalice, of purely spiritual cosmic being, expressed in the dove. Thereby humanity becomes the ruler of spiritual cosmic forces, portrayed in the rainbow. This is only a superficial description of this seal, in which unfathomable depths lie hidden, ready to be revealed to one who allows it work while in devotional meditation.[1]

---

1. From the introduction written for the seals painted by Clara Rettich, which was published by Rudolf Steiner with black and white illustrations in 1907. See "Occult Seals and Columns. Introduction to the Portfolio. 1907" in John Fletcher's *Art Inspired by Rudolf Steiner*, Mercury Arts Publications, U.K., 1987.